THRESHOLDS AND PASSAGES

THRESHOLDS AND PASSAGES

. . . portals to the life you were meant to live

CATHEE A. POULSEN
AND
FRAN LANKFORD

A Division of WINEPRESS PUBLISHING

Scripture quotations are taken from the following versions:

ISBN 13: 978-1-4141-1043-1
ISBN 10: 1-4141-1043-X
Library of Congress Catalog Card Number: 2007904180

DEDICATION

For Mother,
bone of my bone, flesh of my flesh, heart of my heart,
Edith Capece Howell
1912—2001
Finally!

TABLE OF CONTENTS

PART III: NURTURING YOUR NEW LIFE

ACKNOWLEDGMENTS

To thank the literally dozens of people who helped with this project is daunting. We don't want to forget even one. The list of those who read through each chapter tirelessly making suggestions, corrections, and providing copyediting is almost endless, but here goes: Sue Riger, Lola Scobey, Linda Kerr, Janice Elsheimer, Sarah Dorna, Carmen Leal, Jo Beth Viggiano, Helen Hunter, Suzy Scott, Barbara Hattemer, Cynde Elbe, Sandy Gay, Emily Markham, Marsha Putnam, and Don Wiggins.

The patient attention of family members who listened mostly because they love me and thought it would be rude not to at least act interested in this long project are the darlings of my heart. You, Bob, especially have cheered me on, believing in my writing more than I could at times. Your love, prayers, and confidence have been my daily nourishment.

Fran and I want to thank Mick Silva of WaterBrook Press for goading us to kick it up a notch. Your input was the catalyst to propel us beyond our tightly scripted stories to something that would go straight to the heart. Also, our Ya-Yas and other girlfriends who never stopped praying for us or asking how it was going—whether they wanted to know or not.

I want to thank the staff at Kanakuk Kamps for their input in my life from 1995 to 1996. I hope someday God shows you just how much you deposited into this girl's heart. My love and gratitude also go to the pastoral staffs and congregations of both New Hope Ministries and Restoration Church of Naples, Florida. Working alongside some of the best people on earth taught me incredible things about leadership, commitment, and teaching by example. My life was radically changed and more closely shaped to God's image because I rubbed shoulders with you.

The sum of all thanks, however, can only go to the Audience of One, before whom I have purposed to live my life since I met Him at the age of nine. You, Jesus, are the One True Thing, my inspiration, my muse, my love. "For you," as Khaled Hosseini said in *The Kite Runner,* "a thousand times over."

Cathee A. Poulsen
June 27, 2007
Naples, FL

To the countless women who have come into my life in such a variety of ways and made a difference, I love, honor, and thank you. It is because of the lessons learned, examples set, and experiences shared that I can enjoy a rich and rewarding life. You have shaped me into the woman I am today.

To You, Holy Spirit, thank You for the desire You placed within me to share this knowledge with others.

To my husband and dearest friend, you always build me up and make me feel that I can accomplish anything. I truly love you.

Fran Lankford
June 30, 2007
Naples, FL

INTRODUCTION

*She took a step further in — then two or three steps... Then she noticed
there was something crunching under her feet.*
—C.S. Lewis, *The Lion, the Witch, and the Wardrobe*

For many years Fran and I convinced ourselves that our lives were neatly managed and meaningful enough. We were so busy whirling about in margin-less living that even two or three steps away from the tyranny of the familiar left us breathless. We measured our lives by how many more things we could add to the day's "To Do List" without missing a breath.

The occasional, haunting whisper of a voice that intimated we might be missing something that could take our breath away was easily dismissed by the next phone call. We were too entangled in our schedules and the high demands on our time to notice anything crunch under our feet.

But the voice was relentless and persistent. Over the course of many years, and through some of the events recounted in this book, we found ourselves turning from the interstate to a dirt road that led...who knows where? We could only see two or three steps ahead.

THRESHOLDS AND PASSAGES

Thresholds and Passages is both an awakening and an invitation to real life. The life Jesus came to offer is not based on what we do, but on who we are. We are not only wives, mothers, singles, or employees. We are women; women created in His image. This is a book written by women to women (although many men have responded with innate curiosity as to what our book is about). It is a word to those who have outgrown their familiar life horizons and come to a crisis of faith where old emotional blueprints no longer work. In each chapter, you, our reader, will face a choice to walk to the edge of your old life in order to cross a threshold into authentic personhood—to enter that mystical space where everything is different. It's the same place Moses stood as he listened to the voice that addressed him from the blazing bush: "Take off your shoes, Moses. This is holy ground."

This is not a book about felt needs or a treatise on what to believe. It does not offer pat answers but takes a deep and honest look into personal lives with real mistakes and heartaches. It's a book about life and how to live it. It's story-oriented, offering a glimpse into the lives of many who have crossed from predictable, quasi-Christian living into intimate relationship with Christ.

Thresholds and Passages offers a series of portals or passageways to the only life that matters—the one lived in union with our own hearts and the heart of God. Fran and I did not feel the need to cover common subjects found in a majority of well-written Christian books for women: dating, marriage, parenting, body care, and household or employment topics. We have focused more directly on a woman's soul and the call to find and fulfill her purpose, to practice balance and authenticity, to reflect, to play, to celebrate and observe meaningful traditions, and to value the importance of girlfriend relationships. It has a message for all women in any given life setting: married, divorced, single, old, young, employed, retired, with or without children.

This is a woman's pilgrimage of the heart, a journey to find the lost pieces of your soul. Each threshold, gate, doorway, or corridor takes you deeper into the heart of God, who not only finds delight in you but desires to wrench open all the cages inside your heart until you are completely set free to be your own individual self, the person you already are in Christ.

Thresholds encourages your risky curiosity but does not exempt you from trouble or sorrow. Travelers beware. To become a pilgrim of the heart, a woman who surrenders to the summons of Christ, is to encounter dragons lurking just beyond the doorway. It invites you, through Scripture and anecdote, as Jesus did, to count the cost and then press forward. To turn back is to miss the dangerous wonder, the mystery of godliness, and the adventure of a lifetime. Saying "yes" to the beckoning call is to hear the snow crunch and breathe the cold air, to smell the wood smoke and sit in a circle around the fire.

The primary aim of the book is to awaken us all to the beauty, intimacy, and wonder of following Jesus, and to provide inspiration and footpaths that enable us to risk surrender to a Christ who is always good but never predictable. Its purpose is to show, not tell, that life is not measured by the number of breaths we take but by the moments that take our breath away.

It still surprises Fran and me to encounter people at conferences, retreats, or even at social gatherings who tell us, "I'm not seeking something more. I'm thoroughly satisfied with my relationship with Christ." In our thinking, this is akin to standing on the north rim of the Grand Canyon and saying, "Nice hole."

How, we wonder, could we have ever been satisfied with our journey in Christ in light of these words:

> Oh, the depth of the riches both of the wisdom and knowledge of God! How unsearchable are His judgments and His ways past finding out!
>
> —Romans 11:33, NKJV

We happily count ourselves among the dissatisfied—the company of those who seek for more. As long as we can say we haven't yet reached the depth of the riches, wisdom and knowledge that are to be found in Christ, we'll be moving forward on that search. We invite you to come with us, to meet us in the golden sea. It's where we'll be.

PART I

ACHING FOR SOMETHING MORE

CHAPTER 1

STANDING AT THE THRESHOLD
A Defining Moment of Choice

All of us go through life from one threshold to another. And at those thresholds, most of us stand on very tentative legs, wanting to take a step, but we're hesitant, unsure. We wonder what lies ahead? And what has to be left behind in getting there?
—Ken Gire, *Windows of the Soul*[1]

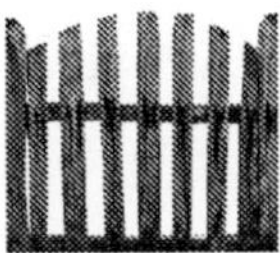

Look! Here I stand at the door and knock. If you hear me calling and open the door, I will come in...
—Revelation 3:20, NLT

We stood in the center of our family room looking at each other, neither of us knowing what to say next. I had just asked Bob a question, and though he answered truthfully, it was the wrong answer. At least it wasn't the answer I wanted to hear. I stared at a little crease in the left sleeve of his otherwise neatly ironed shirt. *How did I miss that?*

I thought. Bob looked down at me from his 6'4" advantage and waited for my response. When none came, he simply walked away.

It's over, I thought. *My marriage is over.* Bob's secret left me stunned, almost as if he'd slapped me. Was it my imagination, or had the ground beneath me just shifted? I kept standing there, waiting, I guess, for things to go back to normal. A little shaft of waning sunlight bounced off the silver frame of our twenty-fifth anniversary photo. There we were, glasses raised, broad grins on our faces. Was that only five years ago?

During the last few difficult years, with finances stretched thin and three teenagers stretching us even further, I had clutched the one stable thing I could trust—my marriage. Bob was my last reassurance that life wouldn't disintegrate around me.

This can't be happening. Surely it isn't true. My husband is not capable of this kind of betrayal. I remembered reading somewhere that if the earth shifts and mountains are plunged into the sea, God will be there with the help we need. A present help, or something like that. *Where are You now, God? Why can't I feel anything?*

Now What?

Bob's disclosure left me rigid with disbelief and paralyzed with the "now what?" syndrome. Processing this world-tilting event differed little from hearing news of a natural disaster or death of a loved one. A wave of nausea, and then a black fog fell that cloistered me from the frightening weight of the moment. I couldn't feel or think. I had no paradigm for this. Icy fingers of dread slipped into my soul as the questions assailed me: *What about our family? Our ministries? How will we face people?* All the pat answers I gave others now fled like scurrying mice on a sinking ship.

A hornet's nest of questions pelted me like missiles aimed at my mind. What had I staked my entire life on? What about the guarantees? What about all those Bible promises? You know the ones: If you read your Bible and pray and go to church whenever there's an opportunity, your life will turn out perfectly. I had believed all this and followed the directive religiously.

God, why didn't You show me? Give me some warning? Why did it have to come to this?

My mind swirled with questions, but the heavens were silent. I felt I couldn't let anyone see that Bob and I actually struggled with sin. We were leaders. This would bring loss of hope to all those whom we had counseled. People might think we weren't committed Christians, or that we weren't mature. We wouldn't be seen as being different from anyone else in this fallen world. Worst of all, people might think that God isn't real or that Jesus doesn't make our lives perfect.

Though I had no idea at the time, God Himself was chipping away at my wall of defense and spiritual pride. It was imperative that I faced these questions. In the past I had focused on doing all the right things the right way, but now I was finally face to face with the truth. Bob's choice tore away the invisible bubble of "safe" Christianity I'd created and in which I'd lived a pleasant life. The screaming question I was left with was the one I'd been quietly stuffing every time I saw a Christian struggle to overcome difficult circumstances: *If something like this could happen to a faithful Christian, what's the point in serving Christ?*

Somehow, in the midst of all this confusion, Bob and I stumbled to our mid-week service. We probably looked like a couple of zombies—soulless bodies walking in a distant haze. Yet while I listened to the message, my mind turned inward, making note of the chaos of my emotions. Something was grabbing at me, sucking me downward into a whirlpool of fear and fury.

Three of my children were adults, and I knew this news would devastate them. Their dad was their hero, their rock in stormy seas. Their image of him would be shattered. My youngest child, a son, was by God's mercy on a mission trip to Mexico at the time Bob shared his story. I looked back later with gratitude at the amazing kindness of the Lord to sequester him from watching the emotional upheaval that took place that week. At the conclusion of the week, Hurricane Andrew hit full force just southeast of us and we experienced 90 mph winds. Our son's mission trip was extended two extra days. Even the timing of the storm seemed symbolic.

At the time this happened, I was leading a monthly women's group of 100 women. Some of my first thoughts went to them. *How would I stand in front of them again? How could I counsel them about their marriages anymore? What would I say about my faith in God's ability to lead us through anything? I'm Cathee, the Dragonslayer. To others I am a woman of great faith who has continued to love and serve God in spite of a daughter who is an addict and has served time in jail. But I'm not sure I can go on now. How can I let these women down, Lord?*

My mind flashed back to a small booklet I had read as a young woman. It was called *The Darling of Your Heart,* and it was the story of Abraham and Isaac. It told how we could love something so deeply that it becomes an idol to us and how, like Abraham, God may ask us to lay our Isaac down.

Thoughts came in waves, often opposing each other as the battle raged in my head. I had been fighting the enemy nose to nose for the past seven years for my daughter's life, but this felt like the death blow. This time, my enemy had shot his razor-sharp arrow right at my Achilles' heel. This was my Isaac, and I didn't want to lay him down.

What do I do now, Lord? What about all those verses I believed for years—the ones with promises and guarantees? Why didn't You keep this from happening? Why? Why? Why?

The Threshold

Fifteen years later, I've come to understand that "why?" is the wrong question. It's usually where we start our journey, but it never takes us to any destination. We must find the courage to move away from that place of demanding an explanation from God and take the next step, the one of simple trust: *Lord, what do You want to show me?*

I didn't understand any of this that night. I had every right to walk away forever. But I didn't want to leave. I loved Bob and I loved

God, even if currently I didn't like either of them. I did understand that whatever I did next was going to influence everything that was to come. I was at a threshold. I see now it was one of the most significant thresholds of my life.

A "threshold" is literally an entry into a new place, a transitional interval beyond which something new will begin. In scientific terms, it is the point at which one substance changes chemically into another.

Everything changed for me at that threshold. While I don't know where the courage came from, my heart told me that backing out was not an option. After three nights of listening to Bob's story, asking questions and getting honest answers, I knew he was ready to make every adjustment required. He wanted to be whole. He did not want a divorce.

I wasn't ready to say yes to Bob. I was still angry and confused, and I wasn't sure what I believed anymore. But my heart wanted to say yes to God—to accept His offer to restore our relationship.

My husband chose to face his sin with openness and integrity. As a result of childhood molestation, he ended up with a lifelong addiction that led to the crisis. His story is for him to tell, but we began our journey to recovery together that week. I say "our" because as a result of this marriage crisis, the shroud under which I'd hidden my pain and loneliness was ripped away. Underneath all the performance and excellence, I discovered Bob wasn't the only broken person badly in need of healing.

Is This All There Is?

Throughout our 30 years of marriage, I believed the Christian myth that if I did all the right things there would be guarantees—that I'd never have kids on drugs or face divorce or financial ruin. By wearing my assigned roles with excellence, I counted on winning favor, position, and admiration. Don't get me wrong; I loved the Lord and truly wanted to serve people, but my own neediness got in the mix. In an attempt to meet those needs, I made service my door to Jesus. I now began to see it was the other way around.

I had confused my performance and service with God's words about losing my life for His sake. *Isn't this what Jesus requires? My best? Didn't He ask me to lose myself for His sake?* It seemed quite clear to me I had done exactly that. I had lost myself. *What more do You want of me, God?*

Months passed and I began to understand that life, even the Christian life, promises no escape from pain and sorrow, no escape from the consequences of poor choices. I also learned that until our deep wounds are healed, we will translate life through those wounds.

There are many promises God gives to His children, but they are all conditional. Every single one. I see now that the only *un*conditional thing I have is God's love and His presence. Those are genuine guarantees. *My love for you is everlasting. I will never leave you, not now, not ever. My presence will go with you.*

I told God I was counting on that. Counting on His presence going with me, just as Moses did when he told God he would only accept the call to go into a new land filled with many enemies if God's presence would lead the way. I knew God loved both of us and that He would not abandon us in our time of deepest need.

In my desperation to keep everything looking normal, I had forgotten that *being* precedes *doing*. Or maybe I had never even known it. A duplicity had crept into my conduct over the years that had caused me to disguise the inner chaos of my heart. That choice had taken me away from the heart of God and into my own self-prescribed performance. Life had lost its vibrancy and joy, and in the darkness, when all other voices were silent, the question that had continued to haunt me was, *Is this all there is?*

I had become a prodigal, though in a different way than my husband. Making the choice to forgive was to cross a liminal space that allowed transformation to begin. In the end, Bob wasn't the only one I had to forgive.

God challenged me to face the truth about myself and my marriage. As I met with counselors over the next two years, I saw that in order to keep our family from disintegrating, I had taken on the roles of fixer, enabler, and controller. My efforts had never changed the reality of our problems, but they had stoked my denial and allowed me to convince myself I was "doing" something. Prior to the threshold moment, I gave myself away piecemeal, like little samples offered in the grocery store, to anyone who needed a bit of me. The entrapment went on for so long I didn't even know who I was anymore. I needed to find my way home.

Do you ever feel lost like this? As if all of life is a riddle that no one can solve? Have you ever wondered if being a Christian really makes any kind of difference? You love God and believe His Word, but your life doesn't seem intrinsically different from anyone else's. The swirl of doubts that seem to hang just beneath your conscious thinking becomes the enemy. When you let the doubts surface into the light of day, they frighten you. You see them as heresies and find it's easier to pretend they aren't there.

Finding the Way Home

In the movie *Dead Poet's Society,* there's a scene in which Professor Keating explains to his class that poetry is not like laying pipe—something that is just reduced to rhyme and meter. His explanation of poetry is a worthy comment on the meaning of life:

> We don't read and write poetry because it's cute. We read and write poetry because we are members of the human race. And the human race is filled with passion. And medicine, law, business, engineering, these are noble pursuits and necessary to sustain life. But poetry, beauty, romance, love, these are what we stay alive for.[2]

In the months following Bob's disclosure, I grappled with the knowledge that my obsession with performance was a disguise. It kept me from seeing how broken I really was. I did not resign my position as leader of the women's ministry, but I stepped aside for three months and let others from my capable team lead the meetings while I put myself under the counsel of those who could help me. Our pastors were completely supportive and felt that God would bring healing to us as we sought help through wise counselors.

In increments of awareness, I began to understand that I had traded poetry, beauty, romance, and love for a tidy circumscribed life. I looked good to the church world—disciplined, faithful, and deeply spiritual—and received the affirmation I craved, the opinion of others that kept my mask in place. None of them had noticed that my joy had slipped—least of all me.

As I came to grips with my lack of authenticity, I decided I didn't like the trade-off. The song had gone out of my soul. The days of wine and roses seemed part of an old daydream. Parents, well-intentioned teachers, and mentors tell us it is a daydream from which we must wake, that dumping the dreams is part of maturity. Most days, I felt more dead than mature. However, as a result of my willingness to surrender control back to God, the sun began to break through the fog. I saw there *is* something that needs to die in us, but it's not the poetry, beauty, and adventure.

What Needs to Die?

Everything in my life and faith was called into question the day Bob disclosed his story to me. Our dream of a ministry together, our future as a godly couple who lived for Christ alone, my expectations of a happy family that exemplified faith in God's Word. It was all shattered in one moment.

I came across the following statement in an Internet newsletter called the *Monday Morning Memo* by Roy H. Williams: "Every dream of the future is a seed. But until your dream falls into the ground and dies, it cannot burst from the ground and deliver the harvest you seek. Is your commitment strong enough to survive the death of your dream? Will you be found *still hanging on* when hope has fled, the room is dark and everyone believes you a fool?"[3] I almost shouted "hooray!" when I read those words.

That is Roy Williams's account of Jesus' statement in John 12:24-25. It's also what I understood as the question God posed to me at this juncture. If I hoped to regain my life with Bob, receive healing for my own brokenness, and receive with arms wide open the magnificent life I was created for, I had to let go of what had been and trust God for what might be. *THE MESSAGE* puts John 12:24-25 this way:

> Listen carefully: Unless a grain of wheat is buried in the ground, dead to the world, it is never any more than a grain of wheat…anyone who holds on to life just as it is destroys that life. But if you let it go, reckless in your love, you'll have it forever, real and eternal.

The cycle of life is birth, death, and resurrection to new life. A portion of my life ended as a result of my surrender to God, but as the grain of my old self fell to the ground and died, something new and precious began to happen. God began to dismantle the prevailing ideas I had blindly followed for years.

Leap and the Net Will Appear

Sometimes, when a new door presents itself to us, we stand before it perplexed and indecisive. We can even stand at that threshold for years, afraid to cross it because in so doing we must let go of the old life that is all we have ever known. We are bound to the tyranny of the familiar and terrified of the unknown that lies ahead.

If it's true that a threshold is a place of transition beyond which some new action is likely to begin, wouldn't it make sense for God to draw us to the edge? We are so much like ordinary hobbits, content to sing songs about others' adventures, while God has invited us to pursue our own. It's so easy to be comfortable and stuck.

Admittedly, walking away from what's familiar can be frightening. We can remain where we are, treading the water of our present life, and then end up where Jesse Sullivan did. In *The Mermaid Chair,* we read her description of her life:

> I lived molded to the smallest space possible, my days the size of little beads that passed without passion through my fingers…at forty-two I'd never done anything that took my own breath away, and I suppose now that was part of the problem—my chronic inability to astonish myself.[4]

We are not created by the hand of God and brought to life by the Spirit's breath to live ho-hum, predictable lives. We are meant to live astonishing lives.

Jesus made some radical assertions in the course of His three-year ministry. Those who heard Him often marveled that no one had ever come along who spoke as He did. One of His most definitive declarations, found in John 10:10, turned out to be something of a mission statement: "I came so they can have real and eternal life, more and better life than they ever dreamed of" (*THE MESSAGE*). This was the first idea to assault my pre-measured, circumscribed way of thinking. In the end, it was the *unasked* question that stumped me. Was John 10:10 a description of *my* life?

Choosing to accept God's offer in John 10:10 doesn't require a crisis. If we've already surrendered to His love, our threshold might be one of new direction or a deeper call to His purpose. For me, it took a crisis. I was standing on top of the high dive, looking into an empty pool while the Lord shouted, "Jump, Cathee. I'll catch you." The funny thing was, I knew He would.

Choices That Define Us

We can't stand there forever staring at the open door. We have to make a choice. Do we want the life that is available to us? The life, as Michael Yaconelli states, of "dangerous wonder, risky curiosity, and wild abandon"? In his book *Dangerous Wonder,* Yaconelli explains this type of life:

> When we reclaim our childlikeness, we stumble upon the presence of God—and we are amazed to find the place all children know about: the place where we once again can hear the whisper of Jesus.... When we find the place of dangerous wonder, our souls come to life and we sense that we are on the brink of a great and mysterious way of life.[5]

Jesus desires to lead us to the brink of choice. He prompts us to venture across a threshold that takes us beyond our wildest imaginations. It's an invitation to walk to the edge. As we approach the door, we notice a small sign that reads, "Proceed at your own risk!" Crossing over assures we can never return to life as usual—at least not with a clear conscience.

What You Do Next Is Entirely Up to You

This book isn't intended to be a self-help guide filled with right principles or a neatly packaged formula that reduces your life to five simple steps to freedom. It comes with one disturbing question that we hope will gnaw at your heart until you decide to seek the answer: How do I pursue the life Jesus came to give me?

You are being chased by the "Hound of Heaven," as Francis Thompson described God in his classic poem by the same name. The One you pursue is already pursuing you. Standing at the entrance of a narrow, rugged gate, He turns and says, "Follow Me."

In order to live the life of dangerous wonder that Jesus pronounced was yours, you must be willing to cross thresholds and enter passages that seem for a season to take you in the opposite direction of your dreams. The novelist E. L. Doctorow associated novel writing with driving a car at night. Even though you can see only as far as your headlights, you can make the whole trip that way. This is an apt description of our journey in Christ.

The path we're on is not revealed all at once. It's impossible to see more than just a few feet ahead to the next bend. Psalm 119:105 tells us that God's Word, His instruction and guidance, is a lamp for our feet and a light for our path. A lamp throws less illumination than a headlight, but it is enough to light the next step, and we can make the whole trip that way.

What you do next is entirely up to you. The invitation has been offered. The door leads away from where you are now, out of your place of comfort and what's most familiar, and into a place of wonder and possibility. It's up to you to respond. Once you say yes, He will show you what happens next.

The door stands ajar.

THE OTHER SIDE OF THE THRESHOLD

The Place of Ruthless Trust

We assume God wants order, conformity—obedient children. Instead, we find that He wants our passionate involvement and utter awe in the mystery of His glorious character…He draws us to the extreme edge of life, where we cannot live by careful, well-planned control. This is where the desert begins. It is where darkness draws us to a realm of desperation and dependence. It is the place where trust can grow. God's passion is to rig our world so that we are compelled to deal with whatever blocks us from being like His glorious Son.
—Dan Allender, *The Cry of the Soul*[6]

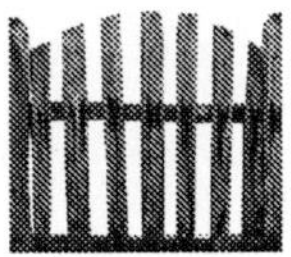

Though He slay me, yet will I trust Him.
—Job *13:15*, NKJV

During the initial months after my marriage crisis, I spent as many hours alone as I could muster. God had coaxed me to the edge, the brink. For a long while, I was terrified of looking over the rim.

Courage comes in odd ways. Sometimes it comes as small gifts packaged in love. For me, the gift came in the form of one particular friend—the only one who knew the whole story. With patience, she led me toward facing the truth and taking steps that were critical to my healing. She gave me the right questions to ask Bob, often reminding me that I would be required to love him in a new way—a way only the Lord could empower me to demonstrate. She sent me beautiful handmade cards with scriptures that went straight to my heart. I felt so unworthy of her sacrificial love, but I dipped into the waters of her acceptance and let them cleanse me from remorse and shame.

My journal became a constant companion. When I was angry, I would pour out my feelings in that safe volume. One entry, made six weeks after Bob's confession, read like this: "From time to time there are flashbacks of memory that bring anger, hurt, heartache, and sadness. But I have been confessing them audibly to the Lord, so Bob knows where I am in all this. He then prays for me, asks forgiveness or whatever is needed. Thus—we seem to be slowly moving on through this period of our lives."

One day, I drew a primitive sketch of a pool of water with a stick figure sinking in the middle. "Help me, I'm drowning," it read. The crude image seemed a better metaphor than a page full of tortured words.

I used to believe my primary job as a Christian writer, speaker, and leader was to answer everyone's questions with a particular Bible verse. What an arrogant idea! Having come to the threshold where my hopes and dreams were dashed and facing the beckoning call of God into a life I'd never even imagined, I began to think differently. I began to understand that the ambiguities of life that haunt the edges of our existence are deliberate on God's part. We can't answer all the questions. Life is mystery. God is mystery. What ever gave me the idea I could distill it all down to chapter and verse?

Rather than destroying our marriage, God was using our current circumstances to rig our world so we were forced to deal with those character flaws that blocked us from being like His glorious Son. I had entered a desert, a wilderness not unlike the one where Jesus met the devil face to face and listened to his false promises. My careful, well-planned control wasn't working, but I could no longer deny that God had rigged my world. And since He couldn't be up to something bad, there was only one other conclusion I could draw.

Rethinking the Scripture

I grew up under King James Christianity. By that, I mean my understanding of some passages was obscured by the formality of the text. Luke 9:24 in the King James Version reads, "Whosoever will save his life shall lose it: but whosoever will lose his life for my sake, the same shall save it." I misunderstood Jesus' words about surrendering myself to His plan. I thought "losing myself" meant I was required to be all things to all people at all times—an assignment at which I labored religiously with little or no dividends.

When the earth beneath my feet shifted and I lost my balance, I finally realized I had spent my life attempting to please others. Jesus does not ask me to give my life to people—at least not in the sense that they own me. Instead, He asks me to give my life to Him—to His plan, His agenda: "If you try to keep your life for yourself, you will lose it. But if you give up your life for me, you will find true life" (Luke 9:24, *NLT*). It's just another way of Him asking me to surrender to His love—to love Him with reckless abandon. I wasn't loving God, or anyone else, with that kind of love. I had to admit to myself that I wasn't God and that I couldn't fix or save myself, let alone anyone else.

In the months that followed, I read all the verses that I'd used to prove to myself that everything was in control. My goal was to read them in newer translations and to practice *lectio divina*, a method of "holy reading" that includes opening inwardly to the scriptures. I began to pray the words and personalize them. As I did, I found myself entering a fresh communion with God that I had never before experienced.

Like Mary when the angel Gabriel told her she would conceive a child by the power of the Holy Spirit, I listened, pondered, and internalized the messages of God. I found it to be a new tool for loving God with all my heart, soul, strength, and might.

Instead of flippantly quoting "and we know that all things work together for good to them that love God" (Romans 8:28, *KJV*), I examined the deeper implication of the words. The connotation goes far beyond the idea that everything turns out as it should. If that were the meaning, what would we say to people who experienced things like the Holocaust?

Reckless Love

It turns out this favorite passage in Romans 8:28 involves loving God with total abandon. Most people don't quote the whole verse, however, but just the first phrase. The remainder reads, "To them that love God, to them who are the called according to his purpose" (*KJV*). It's a conditional promise made to those who have made it their aim to love God above all, thoroughly and completely. It also connotes that this is His promise to anyone who seeks to make God's desires his or her primary purpose in life.

After letting the words soak into my spirit and listening to what God was telling me, that verse became this message: "Cathee, don't you know yet that I can take everything that happens in your life—good and bad—and cause it to work together toward a positive outcome? All you have to do is love Me and make My purpose your top priority."

I became willing to admit that my hope of becoming a perfect wife and mother or having a perfect marriage was more centered in my own needs. When I looked beneath the surface of that glib intention, I didn't like what I found. My motives were not emanating from a pure heart. They were far more the goal of someone starving for respect and admiration than they were of loving God and following His purpose. I was wrapped up in *my* purpose—a purpose born out of hurt from the lost intimacy in my marriage. It became clear the dream of perfection was dead, and I could finally say, "Good riddance!" It wasn't much more than a setup for failure. Once it died, something new and fresh emerged, like the unfolding wings of a newborn Monarch butterfly.

Slowly, the truth came that while my husband had sinned, so had I. I had danced to everyone else's music but the Leader of the Band's. I was like Delia in Jodi Picoult's book *Vanishing Acts,* who said, "Sometimes we find ourselves walking through our lives blindfolded, and we try to deny that we're the ones who securely tied the knot."[7]

For the first time ever, I became willing to untie the knot. I began to experience reckless love, both for Christ and for my husband. When there's nothing left to lose, it's easier to take risks. It was as if I were pushing out of a dark chrysalis within which I had been morphing into my true self. I didn't have to meet everyone's expectations. I could be me! The only thing required was to love God, and from that love would flow the life I'd been meant to live all along.

Facing Denial

Looking back, I am sure there were hints along the way to warn me of approaching rapids. In the rare times I was quiet, an awareness would come that things were out of order. Yet just as reality would drift up from the recesses of my mind, my well-fed denial would squelch the awareness and a voice of fear would say, *If you start digging things up, you might get in deeper than you can handle. Leave it alone. Everything will be all right.*

Recently, a friend learned her husband has been viewing pornographic websites. Checking the temporary files in her computer, she documented proof of his involvement. Twice she's confronted him about it, and twice he's assured her that he has things under control and will stop. She stands at a threshold. If she chooses to face this danger in her marriage relationship, she stands to lose her husband. He's made it clear he doesn't want to talk further about this issue. If she consents to his ultimatum, she'll lose part of herself. She'll become what he wants her to be—a woman in denial who accommodates his sin. Her solution to the problem has been to stop checking the temporary files.

Denial isn't limited to people attending 12 Step Recovery programs. It can tiptoe into our souls on stocking feet until we find ourselves settled in the daily ordinariness of life. An excerpt from a letter written to my daughter, Dori, by a friend taps the depths where many of us have lived for years:

> I'm suffering my fall doldrums, although this time accompanied by a depression even my happy pills aren't putting a dent in. I know I need to pull my head out, smell the roses and all that jazz, but can't seem to do it for more than a day or two. Do you ever look at your life and wonder what the hell went terribly and inexplicably wrong? This is not at all what I imagined I would be doing at this stage of the game. Each year it becomes more and more evident that I have not accomplished any of my dreams or goals. The feeling of time running out is ever present. The feeling I have hidden my light under a bushel basket all these years is prevalent, and yet the fear that there possibly is no light under there is even more prevalent. Maybe I am not the creative genius I have always secretly believed I was? Maybe I am mediocre, God forbid.

The unstated question, the cry of this writer's heart, is, "What happened to the poetry, beauty, and adventure?"

Of necessity, my first steps toward a life of beauty and adventure were steps that led me out of denial. It was a moment of truth one golden fall day as I sat quietly in a nearby park. I bowed my head and prayed, "God, I admit that I don't know how to live my life exclusively for You. I've been living my own life and calling it Christian. I want to know You and enjoy You. I want my marriage to reflect Your love for Your Bride, the Church. This day, I come with the heart of a child and simply commit it all to You. I choose to entrust You with everything that disturbs me, pains me, torments me. Help me start over with Bob. Make it all brand new."

The Gateways of God

I am fascinated with gates, doors, bridges, paths, and streams. Portals of any kind. It isn't so much their shapes or types that draw me as the possibility of what might lie beyond them. They call me on a journey to explore, to find something new, to fall into an adventure. Understandably, then, the idea of Jesus describing Himself as a gate captivates and intrigues me. The very idea of Jesus looking deep into my eyes and saying, "I am the Gate. Anyone who comes into Me will be cared for—will freely go in and out, and find pasture" (John 10:9-10, *THE MESSAGE*) captures my heart.

In His teaching, Jesus often used common objects as metaphors so people would readily understand the idea behind His message. Responding to His invitation to enter the gate is like walking into a corridor that leads to an entirely different way of living. He Himself is the entrance, the gateway to superabundance.

Elsewhere, Jesus drew a word picture of our life's outcome being the result of our choice between two gates: one a wide gate opening to a smooth, spacious road; the other a narrow gate that leads to a difficult road (see Matthew 7:13-14). The less difficult road appears to be the easier way, but when Jesus presents this choice, He goes on to say that in spite of appearances this road ends up in a bad place. It turns into a labyrinthine course of twisted hallways that are dark and joyless. It is the road to death.

The second gate is narrow and the way is difficult, but things are not as they seem. I was confident I was on the right road because Jesus' description was an apt picture of the road I now traveled. In the original language in which this passage was written, this gate depicts a compressed path hemmed in like a narrow gorge between rocks. Nothing about it is inviting. It isn't a white picket fence around a rose garden. Instead, it offers only a paradox. While the second gate is the least likely to be chosen, it is the gate that leads to real life—the life we've always wanted.

Isn't it funny how a narrow, tight, uninviting passage can lead to such luxuriant life?

The last phrase in that verse about the two gates gripped me: "And there are few who find it." I thought, *I wonder who they are—those few? What will it cost me to be one of them?* Risky curiosity began to take hold and lead me on a voyage of wonder.

Have *you* ever wondered why Matthew 7:14 says there are only a few who find the gate? Perhaps it's because not many of us will take the path that is hemmed in like a narrow gorge between rocks. We squeeze in like the camel through the eye of the needle, but what we find on the other side is the beauty, romance, and adventure we thought we were going to lose. Jesus' path to life is always the opposite of what it seems. We laugh with joy when we realize His greatest message is, "It's okay, I'm going with you." He is the pillar of cloud by day; the pillar of fire that burned through the dark to lead Israel through the wilderness. He is the stones that Hansel dropped in the wood so he and his sister could find their way home by moonlight. He is "the way."

As Bob and I began to let God heal our marriage, I noticed a quickening in my heart. It wasn't logical, or even definable, but for a moment there was a catch in my breath and the question, *Could it be possible that what God restores will be better than anything I could have dreamed up in the first place?*

The idea excited me, and I longed for the day that my distrust and anger could be put to a final rest. I could sense that God was calling me to live my life differently—not only to put aside the hurt and anguish, but also to respond to the joy of this new journey. Not only was God going to heal, He was also going to show me who I really was and guide me toward the abandoned parts of myself I had never known or loved.

As Ken Gire explains in his book *Windows of the Soul*, "Whoever it is calling us is calling us by our true name. Whispering to us a secret. Telling us who we are. And showing us what we will be doing with our lives if only we have the eyes to see, the ears to hear, and the faith to follow."[8] Our journey requires us to trust those whispers and to pay attention to the name God calls us.

Hating the Real Enemy

There came a day when I was able to aim my anger in the right direction. One afternoon I lay crossways on the bed, spent from crying and feeling sorry for myself. I thought again about John 10:10 and the maximized life Jesus had promised us. In distress, I cried out, "What happened to my abundant life, Father?"

Once more, I realized I needed to see the whole verse in context. "A thief is only there to steal and kill and destroy. I came so they can have real and eternal life, more and better life than they ever dreamed of" (John 10:10, *THE MESSAGE*). All of a sudden, I started pounding the bed with my fists. "No more!" I shouted at my real enemy. "You will not steal our marriage. You have no authority here. Jesus has all authority, and He will take care of you for me." Hiding my pain had been deeply ingrained into my subconscious by a mother who was taught that tears were a sign of inner weakness. I dumped that lie that day. The tears were a release, and I felt cleansed and empty. Like a prepared vessel waiting to be filled.

I turned an important corner as I realized that God keeps all my tears in a bottle because my sorrow is important to Him (see Psalm 56:8). I am His daughter, and He will protect me from the thief who seeks to destroy it all. He grieves with me and longs for the day when I will trust Him with everything.

I don't remember being angry at God during those months, but I did feel as if He might have forgotten me. I understood that afternoon that my real enemy was the old destroyer, Satan himself. His influence is still in the earth, but I had been given the ability to triumph over him through faith. The closer I stayed to the Shepherd, even hiding in His presence, the less the wolves could see me. I realized that He alone is my protection.

Ruthless Trust

"Ruthless" is an extreme word. It doesn't seem to be the kind of word one would combine with trust, but that is just what Brennan Manning did in his book *Ruthless Trust*.[9] The juxtaposition of the two words is at first startling, because ruthlessness means "without pity." Like Brennan, I'd like to relate it to self-pity. One of the kindest things Jesus did for me early on in my crisis was to set a limit on my self-pity.

Self-pity is our natural reaction to heartache and extended periods of pain. Trying to suppress it through will power just denies our humanity. Besides, it doesn't work. Letting self-pity run without restraint, however, allows it to become cancerous, eating away at our self-esteem and inviting destructive behaviors of isolation such as drinking, drugging, and, ultimately, depression. For a few months, I retreated to my "closet," where I wallowed comfortably in my right to feel sorry for myself. *I've served You all my life and given myself to other people's needs, the work of the church, my own family. And this is what I end up with?*

Four months to the day after Bob's confession (I know this from a journal entry), I sat in my study late one afternoon wrapped in the familiar quilt of hurt, anger, and self-pity. I found myself rehearsing the litany of injustice and falling into the same black hole of despair. I needed a friend to talk to. Someone who wouldn't get buried with me but who would listen and give me wisdom. I couldn't think of anyone I could call.

I don't remember how I ended up reading Leviticus 10, but as I read, a story emerged that captured my full attention. Aaron, Moses' elder brother and the high priest of Israel, was ministering inside the holy place of the Tabernacle. His two older sons entered behind him, toting coals on a brass plate with which to burn incense before the Lord. It seems they brought illegitimate embers procured from a place other than the altar. Profane fire. As these two young men placed the incense on the profane coals, fire from heaven came down and killed them on the spot.

As I processed the horror of what I had read, I thought, *God, I wonder how Aaron must have felt when he stood in that holy place with his two sons dead at his feet? What a ruthless punishment. No grace at all.*

Reading on, I learned that Moses came in and explained to Aaron, "This is what God meant when He said He would not permit anything unholy in His presence." Aaron was required to hold his peace while his dead sons were carried out.

That part of the story was interesting enough, but when I got to the next segment, I began to hear God's voice in what I read. Moses commanded Aaron and his two younger sons (who were sent in to replace the older ones) to neither weep nor mourn their loss. No grieving. Can the self-pity. They were in the Tabernacle to perform a holy service to the Lord. The anointing oil was on them. A similar story in Ezekiel 24:16-18, in which Ezekiel's wife dies and God puts the identical requirement on him, confirmed to me that this was not an isolated oddity.

Looking back through my journal from that period, I found these words recorded on that day's entry:

Bob was My priest, dressed in holy garments and a minister of My word, but he offered strange fire. I have killed that person, partly in answer to your own prayers. I gave you a time to grieve and mourn. I did not deny you entirely, but that time is over. You are not to look back at that dead body. What are you mourning anyway? Get your eyes off yourself, for I have done a mighty, holy thing in your midst. Sing of My mercy and My judgment. Mercy always triumphs over judgment. Rejoice before Me, O daughter, for I have done a glorious thing.

That was the last day I swam in a sucking whirlpool of self-pity. I turned away from rehearsing the injustices of life and began to walk a new road of ruthless trust in a God whose reckless love is willing to subject my comfort to His ultimate glory in us.

Bob and I both made startling discoveries during those years. We truly understood what it meant to be broken and powerless before God. The extravagant love of Jesus drew us to the extreme edge, where we came unglued only to have a gentle hand reach down and lift us from the slogging mess we'd made of our lives. The weathering grace of a redeemer utterly persistent in making all things new led me out of spiritual perfectionism and Bob out of a choking addiction. In addition, He set us free from stifling shame and stale religiosity.

More than 15 years have elapsed since that darkest of nights in my life and marriage. Bob and I are happier today and more filled with the assurance of each other's love than we were when we married. Our road to restoration took time and patience, but we emerged from the complicated maze more whole than ever. Bob was able to make amends with the person who molested him and ask forgiveness of others he had wronged. I was able to forgive and move past my pain and anger. At last, I stood on the other side of the threshold.

CHAPTER 3

STEPPING THROUGH THE OPEN DOOR
The Adventure Begins

Who of us is not afraid of pure space—that breathtaking empty space of an open door?[10]
—Anne Morrow Lindbergh, *Gift from the Sea*

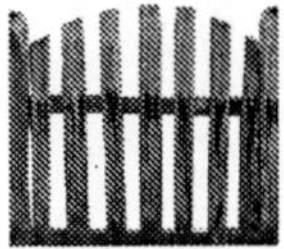

Then I looked, and, oh!—a door open into Heaven…. "Ascend and enter. I'll show you what happens next."
—Revelation 4:1, *THE MESSAGE*

Who of us is not afraid of pure space?" mused Anne Morrow Lindbergh, when, as a mother of six, she arranged to spend one whole month alone on an island at a beach house. She understood how secure we pretend to be in the cages we construct for ourselves. It feels safe in there, and we've learned to adapt to the measured space and keep things tightly managed. When the Emancipator comes and flings wide the door, we are more astonished than anything else and stand there stupefied, not realizing we can walk out of our self-made prisons. We feel instantly transported to the top of a plateau in Montana. So much wide open space. What to do with it all?

Each person reading this book comes with his or her own gilded cage. It's likely you've been standing for some time before the life you long for, attempting to scrape together enough courage to enter the empty space in front of you. The purpose of this book is to enable you to walk bravely through. Granted, the journey you face is spiritual, but it is also entirely practical in that it involves both real-life scenarios and experiences.

It took six years for me to get from the point where I uncovered the false ideas that drove my performance to the place where I was living on purpose. Once I wrote down my purpose, it began to draw me. In mythology, mountains are often symbolic of reaching for the divine. While the mountain is rooted in earth, the peak reaches into the sphere of eternity and draws us upward. This is a spiritual mountain climb. It is an arduous hike to get there, but the exhilaration and joy of finding our significance is the priceless reward.

Threshold Work

Outside of the Word of God and Christ Himself, books have influenced my life more than any one single thing. One day as I met a friend for lunch, she laid a book on the table that had a huge, red bull's-eye on the cover. I picked it up and read the title: *Getting the Right Things Right—Personal Strategies for Reinventing the Life You Want.* It was the first time I ever saw the phrase "reinventing your life." I glanced through the table of contents, as all good bibliophiles do, and I knew right away I wanted to read this book. "Take it," my friend said. "I bought it for you."

Over the next six months, I began what I now call "threshold work." This was the personal investment of time, thought, prayer, and focus that was necessary for me to redirect my life—or, in the words of

Charlie Hedges (the author of the book), to reinvent the life I wanted. As I worked my way through the pages of this book, I learned how to write a life vision. It was based, of course, on already stated directives from God's Word, but also integrated with my dreams, desires, gifts, and abilities. The author helped me see that each of us have a lot more God-given control over our destiny than I had ever considered.

After thinking through the four categories that *Getting the Right Things Right* suggested (passion, purpose, people, and praise), I began the work of rescripting my life. The final draft is called a "vision statement," but it differs from merely positive thinking or self-imposed goals. Rather, it is based on who we are, what we love, what we like doing, and what we believe we are here to accomplish in life. God builds these values into us as a form of guidance from which we can discern our true passions.

On Saturday mornings, I sat in the backyard as pearl-gray mockingbirds blessed me with song in nearby mango trees and thought through the questions in the book. *Am I really doing what I want to do? What changes would make my life more significant? What is good about the life I am now living?*

Answering those questions was a challenge (try it for yourself!). As I thought about the answers, hidden desires began to surface, and the possibility of living a different kind of life began to take shape in my heart.

It cost me something to gain this information about myself—solitude, focus, and determination to find the truth. Once I worked out a vision for my life that was no longer based on obligation and resignation—one that was worth getting up for on Monday morning—I posted it in my journal, on the wall of my office, in my Bible, and in my planning notebook. These declarations began to steer me toward living a life with intention, a life on purpose. A quiet excitement stirred within me.

I had finally begun to *lead* my life, to provide leadership for myself crafted from the knowledge gathered from personal study and from the Word of God. It looked something like this:

Passion: I live every day maximized as a wonderful adventure, understanding that it will be full of surprises good and bad. I am filled with wonder at God's creation, full of thanks for life itself and eager to accept the race that is set before me.

Purpose: I understand who God created me to be and want to develop those gifts and talents He's given me. I work to bring an additional quality of life and beauty, along with a sense of well-being, to my family and home. I study and train and use those gifts and skills to acknowledge, encourage, affirm, love, and minister to others.

People: I regularly focus the best of my talents and love on Bob. Without his love and contribution to my life, I would be impoverished. My love for my children and grandchildren is uniquely expressed to them as my creativity, time, and the Spirit's power enable me. I give quality time to those friends who share my same vision and heart—loving them, giving myself and my energy to their growth, and praying for them. I will also give of my gifts and abilities to touch others with the message of freedom in Christ through teaching, writing, and assisting those I work with.

Praise: I live first for the purpose of bringing praise to God my Father and the Lord Jesus Christ. I sing to Him, read what He's written to me, speak to Him, and spend time with Him. I wait in His presence. He is my passion. He is my life. He is my purpose. I am a worshiper of God.

Vision statements are carefully planned guidelines that lead us toward our best life. Scripting one for yourself will allow you to state how you intend to live every day. It's your unique approach to life and to making your values and dreams a reality. After I finished writing my vision statement, I couldn't help but think of an old favorite verse in Habakkuk, where God's instruction was to "write the vision and engrave it so plainly upon tablets that everyone who passes may be able to read it easily and quickly" (2:2, *AMP*). I had just done that very thing.

I admit that before I could write my declared intentions, I had to work through feelings that this was a form of self-delusion or some fantasy I conjured up to inspire myself. Hedge's book gave me needed permission to dream again and to write statements that defined the life I wanted to live.

Like most women I know, up until this point my focus had been on doing things right. This new focal point was on doing right things. Having experienced five years of marriage healing, that issue was resolved. But here I was, ready for a new script that was based on purpose rather than meeting standards of living that others may set before me. The vision statement provided a way for me to come into full partnership with the Holy Spirit. My outlook shifted away from religious duty toward freedom and joy.

The threshold work gave me the impetus to shift my perspective to what was most important. I had spent a large portion of my days being Martha, the sister in the New Testament who focused on doing everything right. For the first time, I saw why Jesus commended Mary, the other sister. Rather than busying herself with trying to do everything right, Mary chose instead to do the right thing. It reminded me of Stephen Covey, who confessed he had put all his energy into climbing the ladder of success only to discover the ladder was leaning on the wrong wall.

This shift toward what is most important, rather than what is seemingly most urgent, profoundly affected the results I was getting from all my hard work. For instance, as I changed my perspective and embraced life as an adventure, seeing God's plan to place me strategically in the middle of my current circumstances, I got excited about what would happen next. This is the gist of Revelation 4:1: "Ascend and enter. I'll show you what happens next" (*THE MESSAGE*). An adventure is not so much something we seek as it is something that comes to us. This is well illustrated in many classic tales, such as *The Lord of Rings: The*

Fellowship of the Ring, where Sam is struggling to make sense of their journey and says to Frodo, "I wonder what sort of tale we've fallen into, Mr. Frodo?" Again, in the final book of the Narnia series, *The Last Battle,* Jill and Eustace realize they can't run away to a safe place exempt from danger but can only "take the adventure Aslan sends them."

When John saw the open door he describes in Revelation 4, he simultaneously heard a voice that said, "Come on in and I'll show you what happens next." Living our lives with the planned intention to enter into the realm of God's possibilities is like walking into an adventure with our eyes wide open. While we script how we approach the events of our lives, we don't know where the road will lead us. Somehow, that part doesn't matter any more. We know we're finally on the right road! This is not to imply that finding our purpose means radically changing our current life. I still woke up every morning to the same life I had before. What changed was how I approached that life.

Shifting

To begin our own adventure and enter the shifting process, we must face questions that have no doubt haunted us in nighttime hours. While the topic of journaling belongs to another chapter, I will briefly touch on it here to show you how it can be used as a tool in processing the questions that will change you. Purchase a book in which you can record your response to the questions. It matters little if you use an inexpensive black and white composition book, an expensive leather-bound journal, or a laptop notebook. The aim is to record your journey and the shift toward purpose.

Once you have your journal, list the areas in which you feel stuck. This can include money, time, weight, relationships, devotional life, personal character. Honesty is crucial in making the list. If you've noticed anxiety about anything more than once in the past week, write that down. It's possible that it represents a place in which you are stuck.

After you've braved the list, tackle each item and write down your thoughts and feelings about the subject. Thoughts direct our actions, so unless we can identify them, we can't determine the script by which we currently live. For example, how do your thoughts about money make you feel?

Next, let what you've written rest for a few days. Then, when you are in your freshest mental condition, go back and pick out the phrases that reveal your "stuckness":

"I can't…"

"I'll never…"

"It will never change…"

"I have no choice…"

These are the phrases you've rehearsed for years; the judgments you've rendered toward yourself that have kept you imprisoned. This is called "threshold work" because it is what is required to usher you across the threshold and through the open door. Without dispute, it can be a frustrating, agonizing experience. These old scripts are some of the dragons that block your passage to the life you are meant to live.

If you want that life badly enough—if you are tired of what's been your lot over the past years—ask yourself the next series of questions and write down your answers. Take as many days as you need to answer these questions with honesty and personal integrity:

- Do I want a more significant life? Do I want to know my life is counting for something meaningful and measurable?
- Am I willing to do whatever is necessary to become unstuck? (If not, there's not much reason to go further.)
- What is one thing I can do today to start the shift?
- What do I really want?

Now write out a new and detailed script for your life. Don't concern yourself with how or when, just get the dream on paper.

As a result of asking myself these questions and journaling the answers over a period of months, I soon found myself on a journey that did not exempt me from trouble or sorrow but one that encouraged risky curiosity. After all, Jesus never said our world would be trouble free. He said just the opposite: "I've told you all this so that trusting me, you will be unshakable and assured, deeply at peace. In this godless world you will continue to experience difficulties. But take heart! I've conquered the world" (John 16:33, *THE MESSAGE*).

The Search for Purpose

The word "purpose" is a lightning rod today. Life-purpose coaching has become a huge business in the United States, perhaps due in part to our loss of solitude and reading and a choice of life work that revolves more around money than significance. We need direction and yearn to find someone who can point us toward it. Even if we hire a purpose coach, unless that person understands the intention of Almighty God who scooped us from the earth and shaped us into being, he or she can be of little help.

Any search to find our life purpose must begin with the purposes of God. Responding to Jesus' invitation to follow Him preempts all other authorities in our lives. We make the decision about how to approach life, but in yielding to His call, we forego the right to sovereignly direct our own paths. He often places us smack dab in the middle of His highest purpose for us. This doesn't make us robotic slaves, however, cheerlessly running to and fro to do His bidding. In every facet of the Christian life, there is a partnership between us and God. He is ever shaping us, always testing and teaching us—through circumstances, His voice, His Word, our relationships with others, and through our own inner voice. As any good father, our Father desires that we grow and mature—not to the place where we can operate without Him, but where the two of us can be in sync the maximum amount of time.

Purposeful living requires us to live from the inside out. If we attempt to begin our journey without a spiritual connection, we soon discover we are like rudderless ships. We might know where we're headed, but without a rudder, we can't get to where we want to go. We aren't people merely looking for fulfillment or personal satisfaction in our work. We are seeking to make a difference, to live on purpose.

The writer of Revelation further reveals our purpose in 4:11, where we read: "Thou art worthy, O Lord, to receive glory and honor and power: for thou hast created all things, and for thy pleasure they are and were created" (*KJV*). The word translated "pleasure" in the King James Version is a word that is interchangeable with "purpose." God created us for His *purpose,* and here He gives us the amazing news that this act brings Him pleasure.

The Bible is packed with information about purpose. If we are Christ-followers, when we seek to discover why we're here, we must start with the intentional purpose of God.

First Commandment in First Place

In order to understand *our* purpose, we must understand *God's* purpose. He expressed His purpose for us succinctly in simple terms that anyone can walk out: "The most important one," answered Jesus, is this…'Love the Lord your God with all your heart and with all your soul and with all your mind and with all your strength.' The second is this: 'Love your neighbor as yourself.' There is no commandment greater than these" (Mark 12:29-31, *NIV*).

The question we might ask ourselves is, *How personally do I take the First Commandment?* One of the quickest ways to find an honest answer to that question is to ask yourself, *How much of my own income did I invest in carrying out this command last year?* The use of our money is a revealing gauge we can use to measure what we love most.

The deep longing we experience when we are still enough to let it bubble to the surface is rooted in the desire for God Himself. Keeping these two directives uppermost—loving God and loving others—gives us a supreme advantage in discovering our destiny. The journey begins rightly when these are in place.

Exposing False Purposes

As I crafted my vision statement and attempted to live by it, it became clear to me that I had lost a greater part of the dreams God had given me in my youth. Some had dissipated over time, others were hiding under piles of duty and obligation, and some I had rubber-stamped, "impossible!"

During the months of this first threshold work, an opportunity presented itself that I would later understand as a grace gift from God's hand. I was asked to write a syllabus for a seminar our church was designing to help people in our congregation find their purpose. I needed to experience the process myself before I could take others through it, so, with the encouragement and suggestion of the senior staff person over me at the time, I hired a life coach.

Although in my heart I was longing to find my true self again, my intention in hiring the life coach was not for personal discovery. God, however, had more in mind for me than just writing a how-to manual for purpose seekers. The first thing my life coach did was to help me expose the false purpose statements I had come to believe. Writing the vision statement several years earlier had identified roadblocks, but now I unearthed ideas inherited from parents, teachers, and even the Church that had driven me and shaped my actions. These included the following:

- As long as I stay busy and surround myself with people, I'll be okay.
- There's never enough time.
- I don't measure up.
- Everything has to be perfect.
- It's my responsibility to keep everyone happy—in fact, just about everything is my responsibility.
- I'm not there yet.

As I identified these false purposes, I quickly realized they still had me by the throat. Exposing them to the light weakened their hold, though, and as I focused on living my vision and on developing a purpose statement, I began to laugh at the foolishness of each one.

I met with my life coach weekly (more threshold work!). As we uncovered the beliefs that were driving me, layers of performance began to peel away from my life. I felt smaller, stripped, out of control. Then again, I also felt more real than I had in years. It became clear that Jesus wanted to set me free from the slavery of doing things to win the acceptance and approval of others.

False purpose statements are based on fear and survival. Even though my false purpose statements were lies, they ran the show because I believed them. Exposing false purpose statements is similar to how the Wizard of Oz lost his power—once Toto pulled the curtain away, the truth was exposed and everyone could see that the great Wizard was merely a little old man shouting in a microphone.

My false purpose statements were like a screen saver—the default position of my life when I ran on automatic. In order to change my actions, I had to create a statement of purpose that would be the new default.

What about you? Perhaps listing the false purposes that spring to mind as you go about your daily routines will enlighten you to the lies that direct your choices.

Live the Questions

A few years ago, I stumbled on a small book by Rainer Maria Rilke that seemed to be quoted everywhere. I happened upon it as I browsed the aisles of my favorite bookstore, a place to which I often retreated when I was out of sorts with the world and myself. Once you read Rilke's absorbing words in *Letters to a Young Poet*, it's easy to see why he's touched the heartstrings of our wonderings:

I beg you…to be patient toward all that is unsolved in your heart and to try to love the questions themselves like locked rooms and like books that are written in a very foreign tongue. Do not now seek the answers, which cannot be given you because you would not be able to live them. And the point is, to live everything. Live the questions now. Perhaps you will then gradually, without noticing it, live along some distant day into the answer.

Following Jesus is about hearing more than the surface noises of our lives. It is the result of hearing a deeper call—a call that summons us to our true purpose and significance and takes us on a quest to discover the answers to age-old questions. When we embrace the questions themselves—*Who am I? What am I doing with my life? Where am I headed?*—we are responding to that deeper call: a call to examine our lives. When Socrates said "the unexamined life is not worth living," he was suggesting that we learn to love the questions because they define us. Without our willingness to face the questions, we become stuck.

Sometimes the quest for the truth about ourselves doesn't seem worth the risk. Taking an honest look at who we are, or who we've become, can be as frightening as opening the door to a stranger on a night when we're home alone. It might be dangerous or painful. We might stir up old fears and uncover unresolved pieces of our hearts that we tucked away long ago.

Living the questions gives us permission to open locked doors and let our demons out. It silences the demanding voice that says we have to figure things out. We begin to understand the answers won't come until we make peace with the questions.

What are *your* most disturbing questions? Time to get the journal out.

No Shortcuts to Purpose

After reading, answering questions, praying, and journaling, I wrote my purpose statement: "For me, living on purpose means a life of adventure, intimacy, and beauty lived in response to the call of God and in joyful community with others."

Having this purpose statement in writing is a powerful motivator for how I spend my time. It provides necessary focus for my actions. I use my purpose statement as a yardstick by which to measure my answers to the many requests for my time. If I'm asked to do something that does not exemplify my purpose statement, I decline. (Okay, *most* of the time.) I find I can say no with reason now. It resolves much of the guilt.

It may surprise you to notice that a purpose statement doesn't necessarily describe something you do. It's more a reflection of what you value and the core beliefs around which you build your life.

Many fine books on the market today provide help in writing a purpose statement. A few of my favorites are *Getting the Right Things Right,* by Charlie Hedges; *The Path,* by Laurie Beth Jones; *Finding Your Own North Star,* by Martha Beck; and *Seven Habits of Highly Effective People,* by Stephen Covey. The movie *Simon Birch* is also a beautiful portrayal of someone searching for and finding his purpose.

The discovery of God's purpose will require an investment of time, focus, and resources. There are no shortcuts to significance. The quest for purpose is central in much of our greatest literature, the teachings of Jesus, and the yearnings of our own hearts. A decision to follow the suggestions in this chapter—buy a notebook, ask the questions, expose false purposes and the stuck areas, establish a new vision and redirect daily choices—will lead you down the passage into more deliberate living. Making a decision to do the work is pivotal. It is here that true adventure begins.

Secretly, we would all like to have a sense of purpose handed to us, but that rarely happens. While there are some people who seem to be born knowing what they're called to do, the rest of us will find our purpose by deciding to find it.

CHAPTER 4

TWO PATHS CONVERGE
Agreeing on a Path

*And I cannot help glancing back at the two roads...which for so long
seemed to be independent of one another, have just suddenly converged,
and here and now, in a moment, are about to run as one.*
—Pierre Teilhard de Chardin

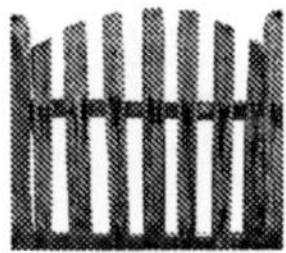

Can two people walk together without agreeing on the direction?
—Amos 3:3-4, NLT

I remember first seeing Fran Lankford on a winter morning as I stood greeting people as they came in for the Sunday service. I was engaged in conversation with someone when out of the corner of my vision I caught sight of a lady with stunning gray hair walking by on the arm of her husband. I wanted to call out, "Sail on, silver girl!" as she passed.

Several months later, after the senior pastor announced my ordination as a teacher of the gospel, I was surprised to learn that this same woman, whom I barely knew, had volunteered to host a reception in my honor. The year was 1999.

Years later, Fran and I could not dismiss the notion that while our paths converged at a major crossroad in our journeys, they also crossed at a significant time in history. The whole world stood on the edge of a new era, and we joined in on tiptoe, hardly recognizing we were falling into Wonderland together.

The shift from doing to being, from ambition to meaning, from the false self to the shimmering authentic self, was subtle. Our transformations were individual and had been in process decades before we met. In the synchronicity of God's timing, the moment arrived when He unveiled a plan for our friendship. If we are to take Psalm 139 seriously, He had it in place before He formed us in our mothers' wombs.

I had recently read *The Sacred Romance*, a book written by John Eldredge and Brent Curtis.[11] While I loved what I read, it wasn't until I picked up the companion workbook that I was able to breathe in the depth of what these two men had discovered about the puzzled longings that reside in our hearts. I thought I would explode if I didn't get to share these discoveries with others, so I offered to lead a small group using their materials. Fran signed up for that class.

Disturbing the Status Quo

To say that we breezed through the workbook questions with glee would be an outright lie. As the leader, I noticed that the further into the study we went, the more people were dropping out. Like flies. The questions infringed on memories tucked away in dark places, yearnings they had never faced, and the reawakening of old dreams. It was disturbing, to say the least, and Fran was one of the participants most deeply stirred. What follows is Fran's description of the narrow passage that led her to consider living life from a different source:

> One evening as I attempted to answer the questions in my workbook,
> a surprising anger rose from within. I threw the workbook across the

room and watched it slide down the wall into a heap in the corner. "Why am I putting myself through this?" I said. "This is agony!"

Even as I sat there, my head in my hands, I realized that some of the answers I'd been searching for so intently were wrapped up in the middle of that agony. A new awareness of my role in this drama of life was peeking out from under the pages of that workbook, almost grinning at me, challenging me to stop throwing up defenses and making excuses and just do the work.

If I had any expectations when I signed up for Cathee's small group, they were to meet new people from church, learn a few good tips about life, and to have a good time. But as we moved through the chapters together, sharing our discoveries openly with one another, I found myself carried to places I had not visited for years—or had never visited. It became clear that I had been drawn to take part in the study by an inner voice that was calling me forward.

Somewhere in the middle of the course, I made the decision to press through the discomfort and see where this road would lead. It was the deepest threshold work I had ever done—remembering scenes from childhood, examining each chapter of my life, letting the questions rise. My heart assured me that in the middle of this I would find the payoff. I could almost feel it coming.

Slowly, as if unwrapping a fragile glass ornament packed in straw, I sensed the hand of God brushing away layers of my old life from around my heart. What was in those layers? Busyness, for one thing. It conveniently covered up my questions and pain. False ideas of responsibility and obligation. The desire for people's attention and approval.

Freedom came slowly, and not without moments of fear. We often don't know how to act when our lives turn down a new road—even when it's a good place, a place where we've longed to be.

Payday finally arrived. Oh, the joy! I allowed God's love to reach inside my heart and heal the wounds. I understood I had stayed busy and sought people's approval because I couldn't see myself accepted in Christ. Once all the darkness was exposed to the light, I simply fell in love with Him. With Jesus. I was like a giddy teenager, blushing when I thought of how much He loves me. Jesus rescued my heart and flung open the doors of my self-made prison. "Will you come with Me? Walk with Me?" I entered into a new kind of relationship with Christ. I finally decided to let Him be the leader and just follow Him. Since then, nothing's been the same.

A Call to Adventure

Fran went on to lead three other groups on *The Sacred Romance*. Each successive study brought a more complete revelation of God's love and His glorious plan to use us in a major drama He calls the Kingdom.

When I received an invitation to conduct a women's retreat in Franklin, North Carolina, I asked Fran if she'd like to accompany me and speak at some of the sessions. She accepted, and as we began to meet on Saturdays to plan the program, a surprise from God overtook us. As we wrote down ideas, brainstorming our agenda, Fran said, "You know, the material we're putting together for this retreat should be in a book."

When we started writing this book, Fran had just turned 64, and I was 62. Well past middle age, we were ready to plan our retirements. Both of us were still busy with full-time careers.

Fran, with 30-plus years in the medical field, managed a busy medical center. She was a consultant and presenter for medical conferences. In 2000 and 2001, she hosted and co-produced a television program called *All About Kids*. Her life was rich with variety, purpose and time spent not only with Bill, her husband of 44 years, but also her three sons and their families.

Nevertheless, just when she began to daydream about leisurely breakfasts on the deck with Bill and lingering visits with grandchildren, the soft voice of God's Spirit began to draw her into a circle of new life challenges that she found difficult to resist. "Reason said I should not change directions at my age," she later recalled, "but the heart has its own reasons, and I could not silence the voice that beckoned me."

I, on the other hand, had just completed my seventh year on staff at a church where I served as the Minister of Small Groups. Although I had worked in churches for 40 years, either as a volunteer or as paid staff, I finally had my dream job. Yet something nudged my heart and suggested that God might have another plan for me.

Rationally, it didn't add up. It never does. Every time the quiet voice of God wriggled its way into my conscious mind, I would try to deny what I was hearing. But the summons came often, usually when I was preoccupied with mundane tasks. Just a simple question: "Is there something more for you than this?"

A Circle around the Fire

I came across a quote by C.S. Lewis recently that brought back the memory of a twilight evening with four friends: "Is any pleasure on earth as great as a circle of Christian friends by a good fire?" [12]

In the waning light, four of us sat around the fire pit at Kate's house by the edge of Haldeman Creek. Fran, Kate, Erma, and I talked about life and about the years we'd felt trapped in other people's ideas of who we should be, orphaned from our true selves. The smell of wood smoke evoked a pensive mood as we watched a snowy egret land on a mangrove limb across the creek. With grace and precision, she stalked an evening snack on her yellow-slippered feet. Everything was quiet except for the snap of burning limbs and dried palm fronds. Kate lit a dozen or so candles that hung in colorful lanterns from low branches all around us. It was a moment we still reflect on with wonder and gratitude.

"What would happen if we decided to live our lives the way they were meant to be lived?" Erma thought out loud, her eyes fixed on the egret. "What if we stopped worrying about everything and decided to trust—you know, trust God, trust things as they unfold in our lives?"

It was a question that would come back to haunt us. The question itself led us to the outskirts of change. The power of it held us spellbound in the moment so that we couldn't speak for some time.

We look back on that night at Haldeman Creek as the place where we saw the threshold. Crossing it would come later. First, we just had to see it. Erma's question invited us to walk to the edge, to probe the claim Jesus made about the life we are called to live when He said, "I came so they can have real and eternal life, more and better life than they ever dreamed of" (John 10:10, *THE MESSAGE*). It was the *unasked* question that stumped us. It forced us to crystallize our intent. "Is John 10:10 a description of the life I am living?"

Erma's question required us to face the truth. From that point on, we could never quite get rid of it. Questions shape us—at least the good ones do—and if we face them squarely and with reverence, they are able to change us.

The Romance of the Gospel

As a result of the evening we spent by the creek with our two friends, during the following months Fran and I began to search for ways to adjust our lives to what we were learning. We talked about the awakening we had experienced during our study of *The Sacred Romance*. We began to view our lives as part of a grand drama being played out on earth, a story where there's a hero and a glorious outcome, a tale in which we have an important role to play. We sensed God's call to follow Him down an unknown path. Eventually, we agreed to step out on what seemed to us to be shaky ground, but we never doubted for a minute that it would be an adventure. All this was necessary to help us make the shift from being workers at church to living the great adventure.

God began dismantling the false beliefs that severed us from our true selves. We had used our creativity and invested our hearts in marriage, motherhood, and church work. Now, our children were living their lives, married and with families. We saw the need to redirect our creative gifts and to make important contributions that went beyond motherhood, marriage, and church work.

Between us, Fran and I had been married for 88 years and had eight children and 16 grandchildren. Even though we'd been active in our churches and volunteered to serve in almost every conceivable type of ministry, we had to admit that something was missing.

Responding to the Call

One morning I stared out my office window as early sunlight filtered through Florida pines and asked the Lord if there was something I should do next. Instantly, a memory flashed to mind of a bridge I'd crossed when I worked at a camp in Missouri.

In that memory, my four-year-old grandson, Jordan, and I had just left the closing ceremonies at the camp that evening and headed for the parking lot. Before I realized where we were, my grandson had led me to the edge of a rope bridge that was suspended high over the road. With childlike confidence, he set out across the bridge like Opie on his way to the Mayberry fishing hole. The moment my foot touched the first board and I felt the bridge move, I froze on the spot. Paralyzed, unable to take another step, I tried to talk Jordan into turning back and taking another route.

"Come on, Gram, it's okay," he said as he skipped out into the middle, the bridge swaying slightly from side to side. "Just follow me." Having a fear of heights, the thought of crossing something that swayed 30 feet in the air terrified me. However, I couldn't let Jordan know how scared I was, so I assured myself that if a four-year-old could do this, so could I. To this day, I don't know how I crossed that rope bridge. I just kept my eyes on Jordan.

Why did that memory come to mind, Lord? God's answer seemed to materialize before me, and I could imagine Him saying, "What I'm calling you to do will make you feel like you did on that rope bridge— frightened, anxious, and ready to turn back. But as I led you across that day, I will lead you now. Will you trust Me to help you walk this new path?"

It was the exact question Erma had asked, only now it was coming from God. *Cathee, will you trust Me?* I resigned my position at the church the following month. In due course, Fran also left her job, and we set out on our journey to write the book and draft initial plans for a women's conference ministry.

The Gateway to Superabundance

When Jesus said, "I am the Gate…anyone who goes through me will be cared for—will freely go in and out, and find pasture" (John 10:9, *THE MESSAGE)*, the idea He was illustrating was that responding to His invitation was like walking through an opening that led to an entirely different way of living. He himself was the entrance or gateway to superabundance.

He continued, "A thief is only there to steal and kill and destroy. I came so they can have real and eternal life, more and better life than they ever dreamed of" (v. 10, *THE MESSAGE*). These words form the core of this book.

Gateways present themselves to us in countless ways. I might pick up a magazine in a doctor's waiting room and be drawn to an ad for an online photography course. Something quickens in the heart—it isn't logical, or even definable, but for a moment there's a catch in my breath and I ask myself, *Could I?* I might get a phone call from my girlfriend who has a wedding for her daughter scheduled. "Guess what?" she says. "The caterer is in the hospital, and we only have two weeks until the wedding. Could you help us?" Instant tears may spring up. How could she have known? I was just asking God this morning where I could use my desire for creative hospitality.

As Ken Gire explains in his book *Windows of the Soul,* "Whoever it is calling us is calling us by our true name. Whispering to us a secret. Telling us who we are. And showing us what we will be doing with our lives if only we have the eyes to see, the ears to hear, and the faith to follow."[13] Our journey requires us to trust those whispers and to pay attention to the name He calls us.

Deciding to Open the Envelope

Such are the callings of God. They often start as small steps that lead to entire life changes. That is how the journey began for Fran and me. As we delved into the claim of Christ found in John 10:10, it became clear this was not religious jargon. It was an engraved invitation with our names on it—an invitation that we couldn't resist opening any longer.

After years of functioning on demand, we had found ourselves empty, lonely, hungry, and tired. How had we lived all those years attempting to please everyone? It was an assignment, we came to realize, that was impossible. We had labored at a life God had never called us to live, taking on tasks He never assigned, in order to be deemed faithful and responsible. Once awakened—a process that, for us, took place over several years—everything changed. In short time, we found we couldn't keep the new discoveries about these truths to ourselves.

The Choice to Move Forward

Together, Fran and I brainstormed the chapter titles and chose the stories we would include in this book. We've collaborated over the phone from a distance of 1,340 miles, thankful we had flat-rate long distance accounts. We've sat at a patio table over cups of steaming coffee on winter Florida mornings, talking, sharing, and deciding what to include and what to cut. As with everything else we're writing about, we've trusted God to put together the parts of the journey that awaken us to the adventure of real life—more and better than we've ever dared to dream.

These first four chapters provide the backdrop that brought us to a place of aching for something more. Living with the longing, facing the questions that haunted us at night, did not feel comfortable or safe. Nevertheless, these were the portals to transition when it came. Our hearts welcomed the change in spite of periodic apprehension.

In the next section of the book, "The Inner Path of Freedom," we move from the threshold and invitation of an open door to the pathways that will allow us to walk in the freedom of new identity. As you read this next section, be gentle and compassionate toward yourself as you approach each new place in the road. Remember that change takes time, courage, knowledge, and a ton of grace. The reward comes as old ways of thinking, feeling, and acting pass away and a fresh morning dawns. It's so good to see the sun come up!

PART II

THE INNER PATH TO WHOLENESS

CHAPTER 5

SAILING THE SEA OF TRANQUILITY
Learning to Navigate by Peace

—Richard Foster, *Celebration of Discipline*[14]

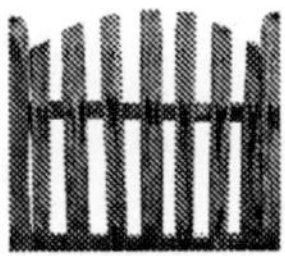

And let the peace of Christ rule in your hearts…
—Colossians 3:15, NASB

Fran shares the following story of how she tried for years to balance everything in her life and "keep her plates spinning," until one day it all came crashing down around her:

"The balancing act extraordinaire!" an announcer cried. I was on the edge of my seat as the young performer on stage placed a dozen thin rods into holes on a table. He proceeded to put plates on top of each rod and give them a twirl. As soon as he had four or five plates twirling, the first few started to wobble. He'd then race back to twirl them again, adding a few more plates to the remaining rods. This nerve-racking exhibition continued until a dozen plates were twirling atop the rods.

"Fran! Get back in your seat!" Mother shouted over the applause. Fascinated with the show, I had inched my way to the railing to see better. At six years of age, nothing was more thrilling than the spinning plates act.

Years later, the balancing act extraordinaire became a picture of my life. I became that performer, trying to keep all the plates spinning, constantly adding new ones as I scurried about caring for a husband and three sons. I can almost hear you say, "Yeah, me too," but I must tell you I carried this assignment to the outer limits of reason.

Hungry for approval and bent on the perfection necessary to win it, I existed for the praise of others. Everyone was delighted with my perfectionism. Why wouldn't they be? They were the ones who received the home-baked cakes and casseroles, the special gifts and notes. Rather than heeding the voice of God, I listened to a voice that continually drove me. I boiled and bleached little white socks and shoelaces until they disintegrated. Once, I over-bleached my husband's canvas tennis shoes, and when he went for a lay-up on the basketball court, he slid right off the soles. My windows had to sparkle like new glass. I even ironed underwear.

My balancing performance act resembled a carefully orchestrated circus sideshow—one like the man with the spinning plates. I could not afford one misstep for fear it would throw everything in my life out of whack. In my eighth year of marriage, it all came to a sudden end. Every plate fell to the floor and crashed in one afternoon.

Through a series of discoveries, I learned my husband was having an affair. As I stared at the evidence in my hand, a paralyzing fear crept into my soul. The betrayal was suffocating, and questions flew around in my head like a swarm of flies. How could this be? Wasn't I the perfect wife and mother?

What Does God Really Want?

Aspects of Fran's story resonate within each of us. The busyness, the striving for perfection and approval, the resulting loss of balance and purpose. At some moment in our lives, we come to realize that those habits are empty and lifeless, producing nothing but more stress. For many the moment comes during a crisis, when they ask the real and honest question: "What does God really want?"

The answer seems to lie in the following words written by Dan Allender in *The Cry of the Soul,* a book about how our emotions reveal our deepest questions about God:

> We assume God wants order, conformity—obedient children. Instead, we find that He wants our passionate involvement and utter awe in the mystery of His glorious character…. He draws us to the extreme edge of life, where we cannot live by careful, well-planned control. This is where the desert begins. It is where darkness draws us to a realm of desperation and dependence. It is the place where trust can grow. God's passion is to rig our world so that we are compelled to deal with whatever blocks us from being like His glorious Son.[15]

I have both loved and hated those words. That God might "rig" our world is not a pleasant thought. In fact, it seems downright heresy to believe that God would lead us to desperation in order to compel us to deal with the things that block us from becoming Christlike. Nevertheless, His highest goal for us is that we should be like His Son. Fran came face to face with a bend in the road that afternoon that led her family in another direction. She continues her story:

> I spent those eight years dashing about, occupied with children, failing to recognize any warning signs or to grapple with deep questions. I assumed my marriage would thrive on its own. As my Shangri-la

collapsed, I realized that not only had I lost a husband, I had also lost myself in the process. How could Bill and I rebuild our shattered lives?

Years later, Bill told me I asked him a question that day that changed everything. He planned to move us back to our hometown where other family members could provide help, and then to leave. After he confessed, I wanted to shame him with accusations, but instead, with God's help, I refrained and asked just one question: "What can I do to save our marriage?"

I don't know how I survived the first two years. I never shared my story with anyone—not my sisters, mother or friends. I didn't feel there was anyone I could tell. It's only now, more than 30 years later, that I see the need of having friends with whom I can share this kind of news. We all need at least one friend that trustworthy, but I didn't know that back in those days. Instead, I just cried and prayed.

We did move back to our hometown, but Bill was unaware that God was getting ready to rig his world. There, in a little church down the street, Bill came to know Jesus in a personal way. As he began to grow in Christ and lead our family spiritually, I began to find out who I was in Christ.

The book of Nehemiah tells of rebuilding the wall around Jerusalem after 60 years of Babylonian captivity. As the Israelites worked to restore the demolished wall, others mocked their efforts. As they walked among the ruins questioning the project, they called out, "Will they revive the stones from the heaps of rubbish—stones that are burned?" (Nehemiah 4:2, NKJV).

It seemed an impossible task. Nothing remained but burned stones. However, that is what the Israelites used for building material. Moreover, it's also how God restored our marriage. He built us back together using the same two wounded people, and this time, instead of seeking our own agendas, plans, and dreams, we learned to submit to the overall purpose of God. As we did, He began to make us more like His glorious Son.

Seeking a New Way

As changes took root, Fran began to look beneath the surface and check in with her own heart. How about you? Do you do that? You are probably quick to help a child in need or fulfill a friend's request—especially if they are hurting. But do you give yourself the same courtesy? Are you a person that matters?

Our God asks us to look inside our own hearts. The psalmist put it this way: "Surely you desire truth in the inner parts; you teach me wisdom in the inmost place" (Psalm 51:6, *NIV*). Finding the secret of a tranquil heart is like discovering a serene pool where we can go when all around us seems to crumble. It is a place in the spirit; a place deep within us from which we draw our strength and courage to face the tests of life.

On our journey to find the meaning of John 10:10, the super-abundant life Jesus offered us as a gift, we have crossed the threshold of decision. We have worked on discovering His purpose for our existence. Now we seek that place of inner peace, which is essential if we are to make the rest of the trip.

The Weapon of Peace

In our ministry travels, Fran and I have encountered women who have faced every conceivable kind of challenge to themselves or to their families: physical, verbal, and sexual abuse; alcoholism and drug addiction; incest; sexual addiction; bankruptcy; job loss; divorce; terminal disease and death. Yet these women have learned to move beyond the suffering—the desperation, disappointment, and devastation—to a place where they have perfect, "complete" peace.

Securing a tranquil heart is not just our only hope of thriving in the midst of chaos and change but our testimony that we know the Prince of Peace. This is not a painless process. It takes focus, deep desire, and unwavering perseverance just to stay on the path to which we are called. Above all, it requires faith in a God who loves us. A God who is good to the core. A God who has invested everything in order for us to have peaceful hearts. Is that who God is to you?

This chapter represents a critical milestone in our journey to the life we were meant to live. If we can apprehend and assimilate these promises so that they are not merely scriptures we've memorized but truths we live by, we will reach a turning point in our lives. Once we can live with perpetual peace guiding us, our enemies will be scattered. Peace becomes a weapon.

The first promise we want to scrutinize is this one: "You will keep him in perfect peace, whose mind is stayed on You, because he trusts in You" (Isaiah 26:3, *NKJV*). God makes many promises to us in his Word, but they are all conditional. They rest on some stipulation that we must meet. In this case, the promise is made to the person whose mind is stayed on God. How is it possible to do that?

A few weeks ago, I received a new shipment of vitamins. When I opened the box, I found a bright yellow rubber band about one-half inch thick with the product's name printed boldly on it in large letters. Puzzled, I picked up the enclosed brochure and read that the company had added the wristband for people to wear as a reminder to take the vitamins for the first few weeks. The company realized that people needed help in establishing a new habit, so they provided this tool for their customers.

Learning to keep our minds centered, or fixed on Christ, is a little like starting a new vitamin regimen. We need to find reminders that work for us. A note on the bathroom mirror; a scripture written and positioned in a prominent place; a string tied around the wrist. It might seem silly, but God honors our efforts to obey His Word.

In bringing our souls to a place of quietness before the Lord, we might say something like this: "Lord Jesus, I am feeling fearful and anxious over ______________ right now. You have promised that perfect peace can be mine if I keep my thoughts centered on You. Please give me the grace to trust You in this circumstance. I choose to rest in all You have promised to provide for me. Worry, fear, and anxiety are sins, and

I refuse those thoughts. Instead, I focus my thoughts on Your goodness, mercy, faithfulness, compassion, and love."

Peace has no counterfeit. When our lives get out of balance, we enter either a storm of emotions or a hurricane of circumstances. We can't fake peace. Either we have it or we don't. Peace, of course, comes from the Person who dwells within us. It is up to each of us to connect with that Person within our center, where all is calm, all is bright. Once we learn to live from that core, we become invincible to our enemies.

Only One Guarantee

The last thing Fran and I want to imply in this book is that the Christian life protects people from suffering. We have tried to be open and transparent to show that in spite of hardships, this life can be good—full and rich with meaning.

In his book *Shattered Dreams,* Larry Crabb speaks to this issue: "The evangelical church has made a serious mistake. For years we've presented Christianity as little more than a means of escaping hell. Knowing Jesus has been reduced to a one-time decision that guarantees the chance to live in a perfect, pain-free world forever."[16]

For those of us who grew up under this paradigm of Christian teaching, it came as a shock when we were called to face divorce, adultery, kids on drugs, suicide, or mental instability. It took years for us to realize that God's Word does not guarantee a perfect, pain-free world. There is, however, one solid take-it-to-the bank guarantee—the assurance that God is always with us, as close as our right hand, and is intimately acquainted with all our ways. Best of all, we are assured of His continual presence and unconditional love. Is there anything better than that?

Larry continues, "Jesus revealed His highest dream for all His followers when in prayer He defined the true abundant life in these words: 'that they may know you, the only true God, and Jesus Christ, whom you have sent' (John 17:3)...It is not primarily about getting saved out of hell and into heaven. It is not primarily about living a certain way that creates fewer problems and makes us feel better about ourselves and our lives. It is about knowing Jesus as the most wonderful person there is, the very best friend anyone could ever have. It is about glorifying God by enjoying Him more than any other source of pleasure."[17]

Believing those words and structuring our lives around those truths changes the way we see everything. If we have made our peace with God and know He is with us, whatever happens next doesn't matter. Our peace is based on His presence, not our circumstances. We're home free. We're safe from disturbance.

The Heart of the Matter

In the small volume *Gift from the Sea,* Anne Morrow Lindbergh recaps the dilemma of every woman:

> How to remain whole in the midst of the distractions of life; how to remain balanced, no matter what centrifugal forces tend to pull one off center; how to remain strong, no matter what shocks come in at the periphery and tend to crack the hub of the wheel.

Most of us know we try to do too much and are weak when it comes to saying no to new requests that tap the limits of our harried lives. Not only do we clutter our closets, but we also clutter our lives. We do not understand that getting things in order starts from the inside out. It would help for us to relax and not try so hard. To try easier. It's a matter of the heart.

Anne goes on to answer the questions she raises earlier:

> But I want first of all—in fact, as an end to these other desires—to be at peace with myself. I want a singleness of eye, a purity of intention, and a central core to my life that will enable me to carry out these obligations and activities as well as I can. I want, in fact—to borrow from the language of the saints—to live "in grace" as much of the time as possible. I am not using this term in a strictly theological sense. By

grace I mean an inner harmony, essentially spiritual, which can be translated into outward harmony.

The answer rests in *being,* not *doing.* We can never *do* enough to make it all right or bring peace to our families and friends by our own strength. How many of us as first-time mothers have walked the floor with a newborn screaming with colic only to find out years later that we were so uptight the baby picked up our tension? We cannot give to others what we do not possess.

Life is complicated, and it is difficult. That isn't going to change. The only thing that can change in this equation is us. God never changes. One of the changes we can make is to seek the things that lead to a tranquil heart and a peaceful spirit.

Holy Leisure

I met a young woman named Debra recently who was preparing to serve as a missionary to France. Debra shared the following story of finding "Otium Sanctum" after years of desperation in a wilderness of her own making and what her life was like before she learned how to have a tranquil heart:

A few years ago, I found myself at the bottom of the proverbial pit with no craters in the walls to help me climb out. I was a senior in college, pretty well depressed, and powerless to control my emotions, my circumstances and my own little world. It was a terrible feeling to be so out of control. I demonstrated a lot of anxiety during this time—panic attacks, not eating and losing weight rapidly, not sleeping well. I started calling in sick to work, but I was more emotionally sick than anything else.

My whole life, people thought of me as a poised young woman with purpose and vision, a call on her life. They said I was special, and I lived for their approval. I believed I was this exceptional, gifted person.

I transferred other people's conditional approval of me to God, and as a result I only felt acceptable with Him when I was successful.

Before long, my illusion of success began to crumble. I could not maintain the level of perfection I put on myself. This brought me so much shame that I began to push people away. I couldn't chance they would find out who I really was. I began to sink under the weight of measuring up to what I thought others expected of me.

After graduating from college, I spent a summer in France. It was there that my mentors took me aside and said, "You are talented and gifted—exceptional, really—but we don't know who the real Debra is. You haven't let us see your heart."

That was a threshold for me. I began to realize I hadn't been fooling anyone. In my effort to build my resume, I had failed at all the most important things.

It took another year of struggle before I started living in Christ's merit. I came to a point where I realized that if I didn't figure out how to calm down, I was going to shrivel up and die.

During this time, with the help of an osteopath who refused to put me on medication but sternly warned me to learn how to reduce the anxiety in my life, I came across Richard Foster's quote about Otium Sanctum: "Otium Sanctum, 'holy leisure.' It refers to a sense of balance in the life, an ability to be at peace through the activities of the day, an ability to rest and take time to enjoy beauty, an ability to pace ourselves…we must pursue 'holy leisure' with a determination that is ruthless to our datebooks."

All of my selfish ambition and the ensuing anxiety was the result of life without reflection, meditation and prayer—a tranquil heart. It was too scary to be alone with my own sins when I wasn't trusting Jesus to cover them. That's the convenience of busyness—its clamor covers the unrest of our souls. The Holy Spirit did not begin His real work repairing my heart until I quieted myself enough to let Him tell me what was wrong.

When I first began to come out of my depression, I found something very soothing about leisurely rituals: taking time to care for myself, light a candle, read a book, breathe a prayer.

Today, it is pure freedom to be able to close my eyes—not to sleep, but to let go and remember where God made His presence known during my day. As I give more of myself over to the eternal order of things, I spend less time defying the world's tyranny of time and activity.

Coming Out of the Wilderness

In this book, Fran and I have shared that we lost ourselves along the path of day-to-day living. Just like Debra, we eventually arrived, disillusioned and tired, at a place that seemed to us like a vast desert, a wilderness. At the time, we didn't realize we were in good company. Moses, Jacob, David, Jesus and Paul all spent time there. It is a place of God's anointing, a mystical land where we are especially able to hear God's clear voice. "Therefore, behold, I will allure her and bring her into the wilderness, and I will speak tenderly…to her heart" (Hosea 2:14, *AMP*).

God actually draws us to that place of barrenness. It's the message found in Dan Allender's quote at the beginning of the chapter. God is rigging our world, drawing us to the edge of life where we are not in control. He is doing this so He can speak to our hearts; so that we'll be desperate enough to listen. What He desires is revealed in this verse from Song of Solomon: "Who is this coming up from the wilderness, leaning upon her beloved" (8:5, *NKJV*).

What Jesus wants more than anything is for us to surrender to Him. He wants us to surrender it all—our relationships, our children's futures, our financial security, our fears about the way we will die—all of it. He wants us to come out of the wilderness leaning on Him, letting go of all else. Peace *with* God is found through Christ. The peace *of* God is the result of trusting Him with it all and letting it all go…which is the subject of the next chapter.

PASSING THROUGH THE EYE OF THE NEEDLE
The Art of Letting Go

So much of the journey forward involves a letting go of all that once brought us life. We turn away from the familiar abiding places of the heart, the false selves we have lived out, the strengths we have used to make a place for ourselves and all our false loves, and we venture forth in our hearts to trace the steps of the One who said, "Follow me."
—Brent Curtis and John Eldredge, *The Sacred Romance*[18]

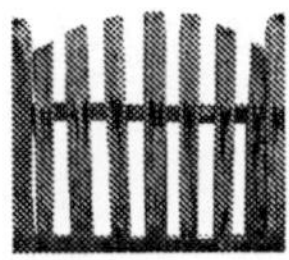

But now I'm letting loose, letting go, like a woman who's having a baby...
—Isaiah 42:14, *THE MESSAGE*

The legend of an "eye of the needle" gate in Jerusalem has circulated among Christians for years. It was believed a narrow gate existed in the wall encircling the city through which a man could pass single-file after dark when the main city gate was closed. The man would have to unpack his camel, which would then drop to its knees in order to pass through the gate. It appears this story was fabricated as an explanation of Jesus' statement, "It is easier for a camel to pass through the eye of a needle, than for a rich man to enter heaven" (Matthew 19:24).

Although the gate doesn't exist, the legend has persisted for centuries, largely because it so beautifully depicts our need to rid ourselves of spare baggage that hinders our journey. Following Jesus requires us to let go.

Even as I write this chapter, I glance at the page of my wall calendar for the month and see this quote: "Man cannot discover new oceans until he has the courage to lose sight of the shore." Clinging to what is familiar, or what we perceive to be "safe," will ensure that we never set sail.

Why do we have such issues with letting go? Could it be we convince ourselves we're in control? Do we believe that holding people and situations in our tightly closed fists keeps things from flying apart? That it keeps *us* from flying apart? The desire to control is our normal human response to fear. In the end, though, control turns out to be only an illusion. We control nothing—not even our own lives. We can resist God and force Him to uncurl our fingers one at a time, or we can choose to open our hand ourselves. It's our call.

Although I heard the first part of the "Serenity Prayer" years ago when my daughter, Texas, was in a drug rehabilitation program, it wasn't until recently that someone handed me a copy of the entire prayer. Although its authorship remains cloudy, it is attributed to Reinhold Niebuhr. The prayer is often associated with recovery (Alcoholics Anonymous has used it for more than 50 years):

> God grant me the serenity
> to accept the things I cannot change,
> Courage to change the things I can,
> And wisdom to know the difference.
> Living one day at a time

> Enjoying one moment at a time
> Accepting hardship as the pathway to peace
> Taking, as Jesus did, this sinful world as it is,
> Not as I would have it
> Trusting that He will make all things right
> If I surrender to His will
> That I may be reasonably happy in this life
> and supremely happy in the next.
> Amen.

The beauty of the words and the wisdom this prayer contains gladdens me. It is a jewel of truth applicable to us all and bespeaks the crux of letting go of things for which we are not responsible. At the same time, the prayer instructs us to accept responsibility where it is required.

Chapter 5 took us to a tranquil sea from which we might gain a peaceful heart. Maintaining that tranquility and walking in it daily requires our understanding of the truths in this prayer. The situations in our lives that we cannot change are endless—our parents, our circumstances of birth, our husband's habits, our adult children's choices, our death, our dysfunctional families of origin. The list goes on ad infinitum.

Accepting What We Cannot Change

According to the prayer, our response to these circumstances is to accept them as reality, just as we would accept the weather or today's date. What grips me about the first sentence in the prayer is the correlation between acceptance and serenity. "Serenity" is another word for tranquility, peacefulness, and calmness. *Could it be possible*, I ask myself, *that my lack of peace is directly related to my constant feeling that I should bring about change in both the people and the circumstances that surround me? Could it possibly be that simple?*

Is letting go of something the same as accepting it? In most cases, it is. There are scads of things we worry about that can't be changed.

Once we awaken to the truth that these things cannot be altered, we are foolish to continue holding on to them. We must learn to accept the following three areas of life as they are:

1. *The past.* It's finished. Why do we keep returning to agonize about what we would have done differently? We can learn from our past, but we cannot change it. There's a marvelous verse in Isaiah, translated with such power in the *Amplified Bible*: "They [the former tyrant masters] are dead, they shall not live and re-appear; they are powerless ghosts, they shall not rise and come back. Therefore You have visited and made an end of them and caused every memory of them [every trace of their supremacy] to perish" (26:14). We need to make peace with our failures, say goodbye to our mistakes, and make a fresh start. It's what the cross is all about.

2. *The passage of time.* Oh, how we bemoan the fleeting days. Our hair turns silver, our teeth change color (no matter how much whitener we use), our thighs become less than sleek, our children grow up and move away, our parents die, and then we realize we're next. Let's admit it: life consists of necessary losses over which we have no control.

3. *The present.* To accept is to surrender to what is before us in this present moment: our circumstances, our job, our finances, our health, our hopes and dreams, and our relationships with others. This amounts to us practicing Hebrews 12:1: "Run with patience the race that is set before us."

In this verse in Hebrews, we are instructed to strip off and throw aside every unnecessary weight in order to run the race to which Jesus calls us. What else is this but letting go? Too often we confuse letting go of these encumbrances with ditching the needy people around us and ignoring our own problems. Like a woman giving birth to a baby, however, it becomes necessary to our wholeness to release those inward burdens we've carried and to become separate from them. If we can grasp the truth packed into this one small verse, it is enough to change our actions for a lifetime:

> Therefore we also, since we are surrounded by so great a cloud of witnesses, let us lay aside every weight, and the sin which so easily ensnares us, and let us run with endurance the race that is set before us.
>
> —Hebrews 12:1, *NKJV*

Those who have gone before us—all the saints listed in Hebrews 11 (and more)—are watching how we run our race. There are throngs of people cheering us on, and since they are watching, we are instructed to put aside the weights that hamper us. These weights are described as sin that clings to us, entangles us, and slows our progress. When we are stubborn and resist God's appointed course, the way becomes thorny and complex because we aren't following Him any longer. We become entangled and quickly find ourselves off course in a ditch.

The Ditch of Codependency

I was in the ditch for three years before I realized it. My daughter, Texas, became a cocaine addict when she was 17. It happened quickly. She is a true addict, one who becomes addicted after the first or second use of the drug. Bob and I tried earnestly to persuade her from the associations that ensnared her, but to no avail. She disappeared for two weeks before we found her living in a city three hours away. Even though we rescued her from that evil environment, she returned there repeatedly, until we had to accept that we had lost our daughter.

We did everything any caring parents would do—sought counseling, put her in programs, held all-night prayer vigils, fasted, begged God to change her and blamed ourselves. There were bright spots of hope when it seemed the tide would turn, but then another tsunami would wash away our hopes.

Over the course of the 22 years we endured this particular race, our understanding of "helping" others changed. We loved our daughter, and though we continued to pray and carried hope in our hearts for her full recovery, we learned to let her run her own race. That race took her in and out of jail; put her in a car accident that nearly took her life and left her with some brain damage; left her with seizures and Hepatitis C; destroyed her marriage, family, self-worth, dignity and purpose; and finally took her to prison. She ran not the race Jesus set before her, but the race in which her choices had trapped her.

Her struggles were painful to watch, and like any other parents, we cried for her and attempted to intervene. Was letting go of her problems easy? What do you think? Did we walk it out perfectly? No, we haven't. Nevertheless, we never handed out bail money, we stopped telling her what to do, and we stopped trying to fix all her mistakes.

"Codependency" was a foreign term to me until I attended a program for parents of children on drugs. It was there I learned I was codependent. I hated the term and swam in a deep pool of denial until my own pain caused me to ask for help. Raw and aching with self-doubt, I opened my heart to the possibility that my daughter wasn't the only one who had a problem. When I was able to recite Step One of the 12 Steps for Codependents—"I admit that I am powerless over other people; my need to be needed and my compulsion to rescue others have made my life unmanageable"—and mean it, I began my journey to wholeness.

There have been years when I lost my footing and slipped back into the ditch. I eventually started a Celebrate Recovery ministry (a Christian 12 Step Program developed by Rick Warren's church in Saddleback, California) just because I needed it myself. I've watched women struggle with their attempts to control their addictions and the addictions of their husbands, children, and friends. There are many of us out there in Christendom. Learning to let go became a matter of life and death. My health and well-being began to crumble in the wake of my involvement in my daughter's tsunami.

Texas is out of prison now and has been drug free for over a year. She is engaged to be married and has been restored to her family and the Lord. She is healthy, happy, and living the life she was meant to live. Her deliverance came, as she says, "When I fell in love with Jesus. You have no idea how much He loves me!"

Texas shares with me often what the Lord is showing her about her past, her pain, and her ability to live in this present moment. Once I let go of the agony of involvement in her problems and realized that this was her journey and her struggle to run the race Jesus had appointed for her, things changed with a swiftness that left me spinning.

It took years for me to admit that I could not fix her, heal her, or persuade her to do what I thought was right. It's a trust issue for me as well: I must choose to believe that God will show Texas the way and that she'll hear and obey. That is strictly between her and God. I chose to love her right in the middle of her mess. I supported her with encouraging words and faith and told her often that I believed she had what it took to make her trip out of hell. I learned to be content with that.

I came across the following prayer years ago when I was begging God to deliver my daughter. This prayer helped put me in a different position—one in which I was no longer a beggar but a mother who confidently believed God would, in His own time, work His plan in her. The prayer continues to comfort me when I feel troubled about someone I love.

PRAYER FOR LETTING GO OF A DEAR ONE ABOUT WHOM I AM CONCERNED

I behold the Christ in you.
I place you lovingly in the care of the Father.
I release you from my anxiety and concern.
I let go of my possessive hold on you.
I am willing to free you to follow the dictates
of your indwelling Lord.

> I am willing to free you to live your life according to
> your best light and understanding.
> Husband, wife, child, friend—I no longer try to
> force my ideas on you, my ways on you.
> I lift my thoughts above you, above the personal level.
> I see you as God sees you, a spiritual being, created in His image,
> and endowed with qualities and abilities that make you needed,
> and important—not only to me, but to God and His larger plan.
> I do not bind you. I no longer believe that you do not have
> the understanding you need in order to meet life.
> I bless you.
> I have faith in you.
> I behold Jesus in you.
> *Anonymous*

The Power of Acceptance

Accepting the past, the passage of time, and our present circumstances cuts our discontent in half. It opens our hearts to trust, surrender, and faith in the goodness of our God. Until we arrive at accepting our lives as they are today, we strive. This pointless striving brings a loss of sanity and serenity—and serenity is the equivalent of emotional sobriety.

Fran and I often encounter women who tell stories of years spent praying for husbands who do not change, or for their mothers to love them when those mothers are not capable of love. Is it possible these women are trying to change something that cannot be changed? If so, that focus can anchor them to a false hope that will prevent spiritual growth. It also can keep the other person from moving forward.

Fran tells of her journey to discover the power of acceptance and the freedom gained in letting go of her youngest son:

I awoke with a start, the phone jarring me from sleep. My husband, Bill, picked up the receiver. When I realized the call was from our son, Billy, a wave of nausea hit me.

Nearly incoherent, Billy sobbed out his story. He'd been mugged and beaten on his way home from a neighborhood bar. I watched as details of the incident seemed to etch tired lines in my husband's face. I could only pick up a word here and there, but I knew we'd have to make plans for rescue. Over the years, we had tried everything to help our son put aside the lifestyle that was ravaging his body, soul and spirit. Questions screamed in my head as old fears assaulted me. My husband prayed with Billy on the phone and encouraged him to go to a hospital for care. "Call us in the morning," he said, and hung up the phone.

I watched as Bill put his head in his hands and wept. I felt nothing at the moment but realized the arrow was on its way to my heart. When it hit, I would go down fast. How many more times would this scenario play out?

Following a restless night, we went for an early morning walk. We'd already discussed plans to help our son, but now we just walked side by side, neither one speaking, each asking the Lord for guidance and wisdom. As I struggled to hear God's voice, a picture began to form in my mind, an instant replay of a scene that took me back to a hospital where I worked years ago. I remembered the scene perfectly.

My shift over, I was leaving the building by way of the emergency room. As I walked down the narrow hallway, I came upon a woman and her small son who was handicapped, walking with a halting gait. I couldn't pass them, so I slowed down to watch. Eventually, they reached the heavy emergency room door. To open it, it was necessary to pull down a bar that crossed the door. The boy was attempting to open the door while his mother stood behind him, holding her purse. I was appalled that she didn't assist him. After several attempts, the door sprung open and the little boy continued out the door. It was all I could do not to say something to the mother or to push past her and help the boy.

As they proceeded into the parking lot, I noticed once again she stood aside and waited as the boy struggled to open the car door. The same feeling of frustration and helplessness flooded me as I watched this mother allow her son to help himself.

Why is this scene coming back now? What are You showing me, God? After sharing the story with Bill, we both realized we were trying to rescue Billy, just as we'd done for years. Our attempts had slowed his progress. We were not only enabling our son but also standing between him and God. That day, we asked God's forgiveness and thanked Him for His faithfulness.

When our son called later, we told him we were sorry this unfortunate accident happened to him but that we knew somehow he would work it out. We assured him of our love and prayers, and then hung up the phone.

That day was the beginning of freedom for us and for Billy. We finally found the courage to let go of the control that hindered all of us in our spiritual growth and emotional health.

Learning to Let Go

In her book *When the Heart Waits,* Sue Monk Kidd says that letting go is "a winding, spiraling process that happens on deep levels." It isn't accomplished in one step, but in many. She continues, "We have within us a deep longing to grow and become a new creature, but we possess an equally strong compulsion to remain the same—to burrow down in our safe, secure places."[19] To face the whole idea of accepting what we cannot change or of letting go of what will ultimately bring us more pain, we must face this ambivalence and make a choice to accept.

Letting Go Is...

To let others do it themselves.
Not to abandon the person, but to disengage from the agony of involvement.
Not to rescue the person from the experience of learning from natural consequences.
To admit the outcome is not in our hands.

Not to care for, but to care about.

To choose to support with prayer and love, but not to fix the problem.

To let others effect their own outcomes without our help.

To accept rather than deny or defend.

To focus on our own faults and failures, not theirs.

To accept that we are able to change only ourselves, so we can stop trying to change others.

To accept each day as it presents itself, not as how we would have it.

To decide to live our own dreams instead of regulating everyone else's.

To not regret the past but love today, which will allow us to grow into the future.

To reject fear of what might happen instead of doubting that God will take care of us.

What Do We Have the Power to Change?

What can we change? The answer to that question is *not much.* Of course, we *say* we have the power to change ourselves, but even that happens only in stages. We can surrender to God, yield ourselves to what we know of His purposes, and turn our will over to Him. He is the one who does the changing, however, and often there are prerequisites such as forgiveness, healing old family issues, or accepting God's timing before that change can occur. It seems the one thing we have complete control over—the thing we often need to change most—is our attitude.

Letting go is not always external or about difficult people with whom we struggle. Much of it involves internal things about ourselves that we need to release. Here is a list of attitudes, conditions, and practices that we can choose to release and ask God to replace with their opposites:

- Shame
- Fear
- Worry

- Denial
- Anger
- Feelings
- Timing
- Being the victim
- Impatience
- Panic
- Perfectionism
- Self-neglect
- Stress
- Negativity
- Need to control
- Self-seeking
- Sadness
- Gossip
- Need to be right
- Self-doubt
- Old beliefs
- What we want

Surrendering Control

Entering the eye of the Needle Gate is the equivalent of surrendering control. Just as the single traveler must dismount, unpack his camel, and walk through the gate with nothing, so true surrender is the gateway to our serenity.

Our fear is that others will view us as passive or weak. We are afraid they will take advantage of us if we accept things too readily. To surrender control of our lives to God is to admit that we don't know everything about everything but God does. Because He is all-knowing and He is love, we can decide to trust Him to lead us in the right direction. Yielding ourselves—our lives—to God's control is the place of perfect peace. What could be safer than aligning with the purpose of a God who created us and loves us to the degree that this God has demonstrated through Christ? On the other hand, if we think this surrender means God will give us a predictable, pain-free existence, we don't yet understand enough about living in a fallen world.

Soon after His resurrection, Jesus encountered Mary Magdalene outside the tomb and said, "Don't cling to me" (John 20:17, *THE MESSAGE*). She was struggling to let go of the Jesus she knew in the flesh. He was changed, but she wanted to cling to the old form. Clinging is the opposite of letting go. Mary's mind could not grapple with the present moment, and she desired to return to the relationship she had with Him in the past. Mary found this circumstance out of her control.

We, too, want to cling to the details and the timing of the desires we place before God. We try so hard to help Him answer our prayers. No doubt it takes us some time to see the paradox that the way to receive is to let go. "If you grasp and cling to life on your terms, you'll lose it, but if you let that life go, you'll get life on God's terms" (Luke 17:33, *THE MESSAGE*).

When we finally understand that the Lord is kind, loving, faithful, and trustworthy, we are able to surrender. This yielding takes us into a wisdom that surpasses our own. Once we yield to things as they are now, as they present themselves, we are exactly where we need to be at this moment in time. We enter a rhythm, a synchronicity of events and resources that we could not have brought about on our own. Our heart's cry becomes, "'Not by might nor by power, but by My Spirit,' says the Lord" (Zechariah 4:6, *NKJV*).

Two Steps Backward to Move Forward

In order to let go of our mental attachment to life as we think it should be, we must do it by stepping back. When we set out we are *seeking*, with most of our attention fixed on what we're trying to make happen. As we release some of our perceived control, we step back a second time to a position of *watching*. We no longer try to force something to happen, although we're still attached to an outcome for which we are waiting. As long as we remain in the seeking and watching mode, we are blind to what is happening at the present moment.

Taking the second step backward brings us to the place in which we finally let go of our perceived expectations and just accept what is in front of us. At the moment we consciously choose that position—that letting go of trying to make things happen or our attachment to an outcome—we allow something new to emerge. In essence, we surrender to the power of the Spirit and decide to trust God with the outcome.

If the concept of trusting a power outside yourself seems threatening, you are not alone. We Christians blithely quote Romans 8:28, assuring ourselves that all things work together for good when we love God, that God is on His throne and that every little thing is right in our world. But let one pebble cause our foot to stumble on the path and we shout, "Where are You, God? I thought You said I could trust You!" God quickly becomes a capricious, uncaring person who is no longer deserving of our trust.

Frederick Buechner tells of a time he parked on Route 30 near his home in New Hampshire, fighting a deep despondency of spirit. As he watched the cars going down the highway, one passed with a single word on the license plate. "'TRUST,' it said, the one word of all the words that at that moment I needed most to hear." That part of his story is enough to encourage almost anyone that God speaks to us right when we need to hear, but that's not the end of it. Several years later, the owner of the plate turned up at Mr. Buechner's house, plate in hand. Buechner tells how this happened:

He'd read my description of the incident somewhere and thought I'd like to have it, even though by then it was considerably the worse for wear, with crumpled edges, the green paint rusted off in places.... He was, as I had guessed, the trust officer in a bank. He was also the un-witting bearer to me not only of that one word of all words, but of the message that, tortuous though our paths through the world are, I was nonetheless by some miracle where I was supposed to be. I had turned up at the right place at the right time. I had been expected.[20]

It is this sort of preplanning that God alone is able to effect in our circumstances. Learning to walk through our journey with this kind of trust places us in the most opportune spot for a life we were created to live—a life equipped with every provision needed exactly when it's needed.

Letting Go and Letting Come

Each time I'm able to surrender to my circumstances, to accept life as it comes, I find a softening taking place in my soul. Every time I purpose to say, "Yes, Lord," to whatever the day may bring, I am able to open up and receive all the goodness and abundance He makes available to me. My acceptance brings relief, and I am released from that cruel tyrant that has long driven me to "do" something. The resistance dissolves, and I relax. My struggle is over, my stress dissipates, and I can focus on what is happening in the present moment. "Before you know it, a sense of God's wholeness, everything coming together for good, will come and settle you down. It's wonderful what happens when Christ displaces worry at the center of your life" (Philippians 4:7, *THE MESSAGE*).

The summer I was eight, my father—who worked in Havana, Cuba, at the time—rented a house in the suburb of Marianao. My mother, sister, and I flew from our home in Miami to Havana to spend three months there.

In the evenings, Mother would read to us—all three of us tucked into a single bed so we could be close to her. That summer we read *Anne of Green Gables*. We delighted in Anne's capers—accidentally dying her hair green, jumping off Diana's roof and breaking her leg, serving too much blackberry cordial when Mrs. Allen (the pastor's wife) came to tea. The chapter my sister, Cheree, and I loved most, however, was "The

Reaper Whose Name Is Death." We begged Mother to read it again and again, sobbing every time as little girls will do.

The story, as I was to discover five years later, was not only about Anne and her antics; it was about me—about growing up, loving, and losing what you love. It was about learning to let go, and how to do so.

At 15, I found myself at Cheree's bedside, caring for her while my exhausted parents slept in the next room. She was dying of cystic fibrosis, and the doctor said we had about 24 hours left. After her death, the memory of that chapter came back, drifting into my foggy thinking as I faced the reality of losing my only sibling. My parents, flooded with their own grief, were not able to help me with mine. When a friend said something funny and I laughed, I was confused, feeling I should remain somber. During the following weeks, I turned for comfort to the book we had both loved.

"It seems like disloyalty to Matthew, somehow, to find pleasure in these things now that he has gone," she said wistfully to Mrs. Allen one evening when they were together in the manse garden. "I miss him so much—all the time—and yet, Mrs. Allen, the world and life seem very beautiful and interesting to me for all. Today Diana said something funny and I found myself laughing. I thought when it happened I could never laugh again. And it somehow seems as if I oughtn't to."

"When Matthew was here he liked to hear you laugh and he liked to know that you found pleasure in the pleasant things around you," said Mrs. Allen gently. "He is just away now; and he likes to know it just the same. I am sure we should not shut our hearts against the healing influences that nature offers us. But I understand your feeling. I think we all experience the same thing. We resent the thought that anything can please us when someone we love is no longer here to share the pleasure with us, and we almost feel as if we were unfaithful to our sorrow when we find our interest in life returning to us."[21]

The knowledge that my feelings were normal was a relief. As I think about it today, I'm awed that God would prepare the way for me to face my sister's death so many years before. He knew that summer we lived in Cuba that one day I would need the example of Anne's loss of Matthew to process my own grief.

In his book *Windows of the Soul,* Ken Gire expresses the substance of letting go: "For all of life is learning when to let go, and how. When to let go of Army men. How to let go of dolls. When to let go of friends and neighborhoods and summer jobs. How to let go of childhood and adolescence. When to let go of the single life. How to let go of your children…someday, how to let go of life itself."[22]

Following Christ through that narrow, compressed gate requires that we relinquish our frantic grip on people, places, and things. It's part of living life on God's terms. When we choose to let go of our agendas, demands, and expectations, we let go of what we think life owes us and allow the life God means for us to come—a life dusted with grace, soaked in His love, and crammed with joy. It is precisely at this crossroad we are ready to become who we really are. That is the subject of our next chapter.

CHAPTER 7

PEERING INTO THE LOOKING GLASS
Becoming Yourself

Now with God's help, I shall become myself.
—Soren Kierkegaard

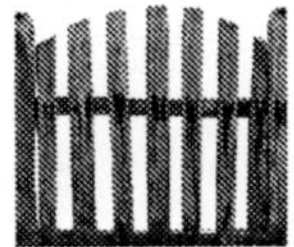

What you're after is truth from the inside out.
Enter me, then; conceive a new, true life.
—Psalm 51:6, *THE MESSAGE*

Do you remember the S&H Green Stamp Catalog? All during the 1950s, 1960s and even into the 1970s, our mothers were rewarded with Sperry and Hutchinson Company Green Stamps for shopping at certain grocery stores. Each month, a new catalog was available with pictures of all kinds of household items from Melmac dinnerware to Libbey stemware. Below each picture was the magic number of booklets, filled with the tiny green stamps, necessary to redeem the prize. My sister and I spent hours pasting stamps into those booklets, dreaming about what we could get with them.

For a period of time, the cover of the S&H Stamp Catalog featured pictures from the Norman Rockwell collection. One afternoon, Mother brought home the new catalog, and on the cover was "Girl at Mirror" (which first appeared on the cover of *The Saturday Evening Post*, March 6, 1954). My eyes fell on that picture and I instantly loved it. For one thing, I wore my hair just as the girl did in the picture—braided and parted down the middle. A preteen myself, I understood the picture intuitively. Mother loved it too and later took it to a shop to be framed. It hung in my bedroom until I left for college. It hangs in my bedroom closet today.

Norman Rockwell, so adept at translating American culture into art, captured the questions, wonder, and fears of growing up in "Girl at Mirror." A young girl of 11 or 12 sits on a wooden stool in front of a mirror, which is propped against a chair, in what appears to be the attic of her home. Perhaps she's gone up there to think things through alone. A closer look reveals a doll thrown aside, and on the floor next to her are her beauty tools: a comb and brush, an opened lipstick, and a small mirror. She's dressed in a plain white slip. In her lap, a magazine lies open to a picture of Jane Russell, a stunning film star of that era. The pensive look on the girl's face is captivating. How does she stack up to what the world deems real beauty? Will she grow up to look like Ms. Russell? Will anyone ever think *she's* beautiful?

Ken Gire, observing this Rockwell picture, summed it up this way:

> The girl is at a threshold in her life, standing on very tentative legs, now sitting. She knows it is a threshold she will have to cross, but she's hesitant, unsure. Her body is tugging at her, pulling her through the door, but something inside is pulling her back.[23]

I was the girl's age when I first saw her on the cover of the S&H Green Stamp Catalog. I identified with her, apprehensive about leaving my Shirley Temple doll behind and trying out the new Tangee lipstick I'd secretly bought at Woolworths.

Many of us grew up trying to fit the image projected from outside ourselves by parents and society. We still do. The false self came to life as soon as someone bribed us to behave with a cookie or a small gift. It didn't take long for us to ask, "What image am I supposed to project? Who do they expect me to be?"

Exposing the Imposter

If you were fortunate enough to have a mother, aunt, or cherished older friend who taught you to be true to yourself, you were blessed beyond most. Was there someone to guide you along the rocky road of adolescence with words of affirmation? Words such as, "I saw you help your sister tie her shoe—you are a thoughtful young lady," or, "I'm so proud of your good attitude when it rained and we couldn't go to the park." One friend remembers a teacher whispering, "If I ever have a little girl, I want her to be just like you."

Few of us ever hear words that pronounce our worth in just being ourselves, so we become imposters in order to get the approval we desperately crave. Imposters overextend themselves in people, projects, and causes and are motivated not by personal commitment but by the fear of not living up to others' expectations. We become what others need or want us to be. After all, we just want everyone to be happy.

The false self is born when as children we are not well loved or are rejected or abandoned. Our young hearts become confused into thinking that if we try harder, others will love us more. The false self is expressed by a compulsive desire to present a perfect image to the world. It becomes obvious that we are not accepted for who we are, so we decide to become someone else. That way, we reason, everybody will admire us and nobody will know us. Our lives soon become a tilt-a-whirl of ups and downs. We rise high on the crest of others' approval and crash to the floor of despair when we're rejected. It's not a fun ride.

God's Word reminds us that our new life in Christ puts an end to the need for acceptance and approval. We can lay the striving for approval aside because "He has made us accepted in the Beloved" (Ephesians 1:6,

NKJV). Could anyone bestow higher approval on us than that—acceptance by Almighty God? Again, the apostle Paul asks a qualifying question in Galatians 1:10 that unsettles those of us still engaged in people-pleasing: "For am I now seeking the favor of men, or of God? Or am I striving to please men? If I were still trying to please men, I would not be a bond-servant of Christ" (*NASB*).

This verse presents us with an either/or proposition: either we seek the favor of God, or we seek the approval of man. One brings us before a loving Father who already approves of us; the other drives us to the hopeless task of pleasing people.

Reconnecting with Yourself

When we come to Jesus for restoration, He finds the lost parts of our true self—the parts that were scattered and never affirmed—and He brings them back together to form a whole. This is not accomplished in the twinkling of an eye; it is an ongoing process of healing that happens from the inside out.

We live in a world designed to keep us from our true self; therefore, it is of central importance that once we have invited Jesus into the core of our being, we invite Him to live *His* life out of the core of our being. This is the incarnational reality of Christ. Here's the equation: Us + Christ = True Self. When we live true to the Christ within, we are living out our truest self, our authentic self. When we live according to the image of the outside world, we live by the power of our false self.

The apostle Paul explained it like this: "Do not conform any longer to the pattern of this world, but be transformed by the renewing of your mind" (Romans 12:2, *NIV*). In other words, we should not be shaped into the world's image but be reshaped from the inside by the power of God. For many of us, the process is lengthy.

"You were taught, with regard to your former way of life, to put off your *old self*, which is being corrupted by its deceitful desires; to be made new in the attitude of your minds; and to put on the *new self* created to be like God in true righteousness and holiness" (Ephesians 4:22-24, NIV, emphasis mine). In Christ, we now possess the power of choice. We can choose to live from the resources of the old way, or we can wake up to the glorious splendor of fresh-brewed life, the choice to live from our true self. When we source our life in Christ, we are on the road to authenticity.

Becoming Ourselves

In my case, it's taken almost a lifetime to appropriate these truths. Through a series of events that took place in the decade of my fifties, Jesus began to show me how I had lost my "Cathee-ness," my core identity. Oh, I wore my roles with skill and style. I was a faithful wife, committed mother, capable administrator, and an interesting speaker and teacher. "But what happened to the girl in the mirror?" He asked. "How did that simple, sweet, fun-loving girl disappear? She dared to take risks, she lived in the moment, she danced to My music. Where is she?"

I hadn't a clue. I never noticed she was gone. Over the years, I had just morphed into a composite of what others expected of me. An unrest was growing in my heart, and I needed answers. Always one to question life and what it means, a place began to open within my soul that prepared me for God's next move.

Living in Branson, Missouri, at the time, I sought the counsel of a Christian woman, who became my spiritual director. Through conversation and prayer, she led me to picture myself standing with my sister at the foot of the cross. We were dressed alike in our green plaid dresses that Mother had made, holding hands—Cathee and Cheree.

As I pictured us standing there together, it was as if a veil began to dissolve and I saw that my identity had been interwoven with my sister in an unnatural way. When she died, I had made a valiant attempt to make up for her loss by imitating her behavior. I began to keep up my room with scrupulous detail. I worked with more diligence at school assignments. I took on chores at home that had been hers. Anyone looking on would have commented on my thoughtfulness, which is exactly what I was seeking. I wanted attention and approval. My parents, lost in grief, had forgotten I existed. The imposter had taken over my life. I never let Cheree go—I became Cheree. What I did let go of was my own carefree, fun-loving personality.

That day, my counselor led me through a prayer that set me free to become my true self. After asking me to picture myself standing at the foot of the cross with Cheree, she said, "Now, I want you to let go of Cheree's hand and watch her go up to Jesus." Hearing the instruction, I felt as dead as a stone. Nothing in me responded. She repeated the request, and I began to sob. Letting go seemed irresponsible. I was my sister's keeper. If I let go, we'd all forget her. As I sat in that miserable place, the real fear of my heart began to drift to the surface of my mind: who would I be without Cheree?

Our imaginations are amazing gifts from God. We are warned not to use vain imaginations, but at this moment, the Holy Spirit was helping me "see" by using my imagination in a godly way. Slowly, deliberately, I opened my hand and watched Cheree walk away from me and up to Jesus. I didn't hear an audible voice (as Adrian Rogers said, "It was louder than that!"), but it seemed as if Jesus looked at me and said, "You are now Cathleen," which is my legal name. I understood that to be my true self. It's the name the Lord calls me.

Despite the tears, a lightness and joy came over me that remain to this day. I had assumed my sister's identity and lost my own for 36 years, but in one prayer session it was lifted from my shoulders. God's timing is always perfect.

Riding the Gator

Not long afterward, I experienced something that confirmed the return of my true self. I accepted a position working for the executive director of Kanakuk Kamps, the largest Christian Sports Camp in

America. Jim Behling (JB), my boss, exuded joy, freedom, and spontaneity like no one I'd ever known.

My first week at Kanakuk (everything at Kanakuk starts with a "K"), JB was directing a program at K-Kountry, the camp just south of the executive offices where I worked. The day before, he had taken me on a tour of the facilities in the "Gator," a small 18-horsepower, three-cylinder utility vehicle made by the John Deere company. It looked like a tiny pickup truck, but it was open like a tractor. We followed a path through Ozark-wooded land and came out at K-Kountry Kamp. That was Monday.

Tuesday morning I sat in front of my computer, setting up document files and arranging my work area, when the phone rang. It was JB. "Cathee," he said, "get the registration forms and bring them to me in the Gator. It's outside your office."

I squirmed in my desk chair. I didn't want to tell my new boss I couldn't obey his request. "But, JB," I finally said, "I don't know how to drive the Gator."

It wasn't that the vehicle itself was threatening; the threat was doing something with which I was unfamiliar. JB, not being one to be easily persuaded by anyone's reluctance to try something new (he had spent his life encouraging kids to take new challenges), said, "Of course you do. Just get a counselor to show you how to turn it on and come over."

Before I could say anything else, he hung up. So I found a camp counselor, who turned the key that was already in the ignition of the waiting Gator. "There you go," he said. Embarrassed that a simple request could cause such intimidation, I gave him a weak smile and climbed in.

At first, I crept toward the woodland path that led to K-Kountry Kamp. Once I was away from the eyes of those who might be watching—I'm almost certain no one was—I went a bit faster. As I got into the woods, I noticed shafts of sunlight streaming through the tall elms and oaks around me. For a moment, it seemed I was in an enchanted forest.

My heart swelled with the beauty of the moment. I went faster, my hair flying in the breeze, feeling like I had in my carefree childhood. Tears began to flow, and in an instant I knew I had just reconnected with the true Cathee, the authentic Cathleen. She had been lost for years in duty and obligation—faithfully carrying out her assignments but not tasting the joy of life.

Looking back, I see that day as a turning point. I wasn't only riding the Gator to the camp next door; I was setting out on the greatest adventure of all—becoming real.

Mirror, Mirror on the Wall

Early on, as little girls, we become fascinated with the mirror. We preen in front of it, dressed in our mother's hats, gloves, and shoes. We delight in our image as we twirl around in our Sunday best. Fran remembers, "When I was eight, my father made me the most wonderful kidney-shaped dressing table, which Mother dressed with a ruffled skirt sewn from delicate organza. Over it she hung a round mirror, rosebuds painted around the edge, and Dad crafted a nail keg into a bench where I sat dreaming up all kinds of things about myself. So began my love affair with the looking glass."

In some way none of us can explain, we become what we look at. We all know friends who were children of alcoholic parents and who made vows to never be like their parents. The wounds of childhood became their focus, and eventually they grew up to be what they vowed never to be. They became the image they beheld.

There's a strange pull toward the images we place in front of us. That is the idea behind "Girl at Mirror." She gazes wistfully at Jane Russell, hoping that if she looks hard and long enough, she'll become like the image she is focusing on.

God's Word both understands and confirms this truth: "But we all, with unveiled face, beholding as in a mirror the glory of the Lord, are being transformed into the same image from glory to glory, just as by the Spirit of the Lord" (2 Corinthians 3:18, *NKJV*). This chapter in 2 Corinthians speaks of our belief in Christ as though it brings an "unveiling." As we look upon Him through His Word—through trusting in His care for us—it's as though we are beholding His glory in a mirror. The more we look at it, the more we are transformed into His likeness. Who we are trying to be falls away, and because we focus on Him, we become like Him.

Cracking the Shell

I was walking through my yard early one morning when a papery, silvery object caught my eye. Caught on a piece of pine bark, it shimmered in the sun. As I bent down to examine it more closely, I realized it was a lizard skin. I've often told my husband that if we named our street, we should call it "Leaping Lizards Lane," because lizards are all over the place. It's part of living in the subtropics. Lizards molt every season. They shed their old dry skins and *voila!* Out comes a new shiny green one.

We also enter molting, shedding and sloughing-off times more than once in our lives. Rebirth is part of our journey. The seed of our true self, the core of our being, must be uncovered.

Recently, I received the following email from a close friend in which she shared a recent experience with a group of friends:

Our group of three had a meeting this afternoon. The purpose of our group is to align with the Holy Spirit in evoking and supporting the authentic self. We have been "at it" over three years now, and we are all standing at major thresholds. There were many tears. It is amazing how many layers of the onion you can peel off, and yet…there is still a thick husk near the center, surrounding that core kernel of our being where the vital seed of life and freedom lies—Christ, indeed. I think we are all feeling this thick inner layer—the last defense and bulwark of the false self often laid down in childhood—beginning to crack.

Meister Eckhart, a German philosopher and mystic, made a similar statement I came across not long ago: "The shell must be cracked apart if what is in it is to come out, for if you want the kernel, you must break the shell." If we are to "grow up in every way…into Christ," as Ephesians 4:15 says, there must be within each of us a true seed. It is from this seed that transformation comes forth. The seed is the God-image that is being regenerated in us by the Holy Spirit.

Unmasking the True Self

My own final bulwark of defense began to crack open in the fall of 2004. It was a pivotal year in that I had turned 60 in May and was soon to celebrate my fortieth wedding anniversary. If I'd been alert, I would have seen it coming. Looking back I realize it was the perfect way to close that year, but at the time I was oblivious to the gorge just ahead.

In order to tell the story properly, I must go back to 1963 when, at the age of 20, I became pregnant and was not married. Bob was in the Army, stationed in Germany, and although we had not seen each other in 18 months, we wrote back and forth about our desire to get married once he returned home. It is not my place here to justify or even explain my situation other than to say I was foolish and careless in how I conducted myself in the six months prior to Bob's return. Once I realized my dilemma, I felt my only recourse was to write Bob, tell him my situation, and place my baby up for adoption. The most difficult part of all was that I felt I couldn't tell my parents about my situation. When Cheree died, just five years before, they had lost their only other child. I felt I could not face dishonoring them with what I had done.

Bob returned at the end of July, and in spite of his knowledge of my pregnancy, he married me in September. We left immediately for California and made arrangements with a physician to place the baby for adoption at birth. My husband was supportive, loving, and even willing to keep the baby. I nevertheless felt I had no recourse but to put the baby up for adoption.

The Pink Kimono

During the months of waiting, I was alone and in a place where I knew no one. One weekend, I asked Bob to take me to a fabric store, where I purchased one half yard of pink flannel. Never questioning, he drove me to the store, and I made my purchase.

While he was at work, I made a pattern for a baby kimono out of a brown paper bag and used it to cut the flannel. I had no sewing machine, so I stitched it by hand and used a scrap of pink ribbon to trim the raw edges. Then I carefully stitched tiny rosebuds on the front, using scarlet and green embroidery thread for the buds and leaves. In the back of the neck, I attached one of the leftover labels from my college days, cutting off "Howell" (my maiden name) and keeping "Cathee." I quietly tucked the kimono away in my lingerie drawer.

I gave birth to a beautiful baby girl in the winter of 1964. Three days later, with all the arrangements completed for her to be placed with a family, I left the hospital with empty arms and an empty heart. Looking back now, it seems I must have gone through the ache of separation with a rigid determination, spawned by my belief that I had no other choice. I simply closed the door on the whole episode, moved back to Florida, and made a new life without her. Packed in my suitcase, though, was the pink kimono.

The Wilderness Ends

Forty years passed. From time to time, I would come across the little pink garment stuck in the back of a drawer. I thought of throwing it away, but I just couldn't bring myself to do it. It was my only link to the child I had given up for adoption, and I couldn't part with it.

In September of 2004, my daughter-in-law, Dorothy, said to me, "Mom, don't you want to know your daughter? Your parents are both gone now, and we want to meet her." All four siblings had talked among themselves and wanted me to take this step, but they knew it had to be my decision. I had shared my story with them years before as each came of age. Dorothy had been like a border collie for years, nipping at the heels of my heart with her questions. These questions frightened me. I never entertained them for long for fear of having no reasonable answer to what I thought would be my daughter's inevitable question: "How could you give away your own child?"

One evening, I slipped into my study and turned on the computer. With a feeling similar to jumping out of a plane without a parachute, I went to Yahoo.com and in the little blank square typed: "adopted child + birth parent." I had no instructions, no prior knowledge about how to find a missing person, but I could feel a presence leading me. I clicked the search button and closed my eyes while it loaded the sites.

When I looked I saw a page of website listings, but my eyes fell immediately on a mutual consent registry. I went to it, clicked on the state of birth—California—and began to realize within moments that I hardly knew the answers to any of the questions listed on the site. I could not remember the doctor's name, the hospital or city of the birth (it was a few miles away from where I lived). I did not even remember the exact birth date.

I answered what questions I could, closed everything down, and didn't say a word to anyone about it. The following morning when I checked my email, there was a message from a woman who called herself a "search angel." "If your maiden name is *Howell*," the message said, "your daughter was born on February 11, 1964." The search angel encouraged me to keep looking and said she would do the same.

A month passed with no news. I was distracted by other family issues and still reluctant to open Pandora's Box. I heard from Judy, the search angel, once during that time, and she advised me to send for a reverse birth certificate, which would give me the name my baby was given at birth and her adopted mother's maiden name. These were key pieces of information. I wrote back that I would let her know when I was ready to order it and busied myself with holiday plans.

Bridging a Wide and Deep Chasm

During the ensuing weeks, I felt vulnerable and anxious. I shared my search with my Ya-Ya sisters and my small group. Everyone was excited and waiting on tiptoes for any news. I was scared. Part of me didn't want everyone to know about this part of my life. While I knew I was forgiven, it felt too private to put on what felt like national television. Like a turtle crossing the highway and looking up to see a Mack truck bearing down on her, I drew back into the comfortable darkness of my shell and waited for the collision.

One afternoon toward the end of November, I came across these words by John Eldredge: "At this place on our journey, we face a wide and deep chasm that refuses us passage through self-effort. And it is God's intention to use this place to eradicate the final heart walls and obstacles that separate us from him."[24]

What happened next had nothing to do with self-effort. It was as though a great eagle swooped down from the heavens and allowed me to climb on his back as he carried me through the wide and deep chasm. Jesus came not only to save us from sin and destruction but also to save us from ourselves. He understood what I did not at the time—that I had erected a heart wall that separated me from Him, from my daughter, and from others. For years when someone asked how many children I had, I would answer "four," and the wall would go up a little higher. My heart knew the answer was "five," but the explanation was just too long. It all seemed far too complicated to unravel.

On Saturday, December 4, 2004, I attended a Christmas banquet at our church. A young woman who knew of my search approached me as soon as I entered the building that evening. She took my hand and placed a wad of bills in it. "Here!" she said. "Order the reverse birth certificate."

I attempted to decline her offer, feeling ashamed to take her money when I knew she lived on a tight budget. In that moment, however, I saw I'd been dragging my feet regarding the search and that this gesture was

God's way of nudging me forward. I knew He was rigging my world. I thanked her and made a mental note to contact Judy the next Tuesday when I came to my office. I could have emailed her the next morning, but I was still pushing the task as far ahead as possible.

Things happened quickly after that. It was the catalyst that propelled me to the edge of the chasm. I started the search process in September, but when my fears brought me to an impasse, God took over. Late in the afternoon on that next Tuesday, I emailed Judy to say I was ready to do the reverse birth certificate search. Moments later, I was heading home with plans for dinner with some of Bob's old high school friends.

Just before I left for dinner, I checked my email and saw a reply from Judy. "I think I have your daughter's contact information. I don't know how current it is, but I'll try to call her. Stay tuned."

While the dinner at a seafood restaurant on Marco Island was lovely, I had trouble concentrating. The second we arrived home, I dashed to the computer to check my messages. There was one from Judy.

"I called your daughter's house, but was unable to make contact. I'll check later." By then it was 11 P.M. and I was ready for bed. *Maybe tomorrow is the day I will find her,* I thought before I drifted off to a restless sleep. The next morning, December 10, I jumped out of bed and didn't even wash my face or brush my teeth. There were just two email messages in my mailbox:

Cathee,

I just spoke to your daughter on the phone! Her name is Dorene (Dori) E. (Coates) Stier. I gave her your email address and she is planning to write to you. Her email is: xxxx@xxxx. Please let me know if I can do anything further. I truly share your excitement and joy!

Kind regards,

Judy

Hi Cathee,

I was in contact with Judy today. She told me that you have been looking for me. You can reach me at this email address (xxxx@xxxx) if you would like to talk.

Dori Stier

With Bob and Texas leaning over my shoulders, I stared at the screen as tears spilled out and down my face. *Where do I begin? What do I write back?* It seemed she only wanted to "talk" through email, but I was more than happy to comply with that.

We emailed back and forth six times that day, doing little else. I opened a new folder in my computer to save all our correspondence and labeled it "Dori—Found at Last." The eagle had carried me over the chasm, and now I was soaring. Within days, Dori had spoken with all four of her siblings, and they had progressed to arguing over things such as who makes the best black beans. Two days before Christmas, a package arrived from Dori. When we opened our traditional one gift on Christmas Eve, that was the one I chose. Inside I found a photo album with Dori's baby pictures and other pictures that took me through her high school graduation. Inside the back cover was a blank 5 x 7 mat. Under it she had written, "Our Picture." On Christmas Day, I made the first phone call. We were both ready by then.

Finding Dori—Finding Me

On January 22, 2005, 13 members of my family waited in the Southwest Regional airport for Dori's arrival. We carried signs with a picture of the blue parrot fish named Dori from the movie *Finding Nemo*, only our signs read: "Finding Dori." As she walked toward us at the American Airlines gate, flanked by curious flight attendants, the words written by a friend in an email the night before came flooding back:

All the energy of not touching or holding 40 years ago has accumulated over time and is now an even greater pearl of great worth the Lord hand-delivers to you. Imagine the racket in heaven Saturday night when angels fill the concourse, the din of flapping wings joining in hundred-part harmony of song, and it all rises from the ashes as Dori walks that birth canal between the plane and your arms.

Nothing could describe the moment better. All time and space suspended as I reached for her, my daughter whom I had not touched for 40 years. I had bridged the chasm. The heart-walls that separated me from Dori, from a relationship with my true self and from God, dissolved in a heap at my feet. At last, I had become myself.

The final joy was to sit on the bed with her the night before she returned home and tell her the story of the pink kimono. We recapped with wonder how our journeys had now come full circle and that at last our roads had converged. Then I placed the garment in her hands, where it rightfully belonged.

Liking the Person I Really Am

How we live our lives is the story we tell the world about ourselves. It reflects what we believe about our Beloved, our Lord; it is what our children will remember when we're gone. When we hide behind the false self—a self we've constructed so the world will find us more acceptable—we sever ourselves from our own creative gifts and our authenticity. Dismantling the ideas we've blindly followed, though a painful and risky task, is worth the struggle. Like Jacob at Peniel, we wrestle with the angel and come away with a limp and a new name.

Our other names—the old ones like "overachiever," "performer," "approval-addict," "Cinderella," "good girl," "people pleaser," "perfectionist," "Pharisee"—do not reflect the nature of the God we love and serve. Others cannot know Him when we hide behind masks.

In her book *When the Heart Waits,* about answering life's sacred questions, Sue Monk Kidd puts coming to terms with the truth about ourselves in perspective: "In naming the many patterns of our false selves…we need to…bend down to the broken, horrible faces in ourselves and kiss each one."[25]

The answer is not to loathe those parts of ourselves or to reject them. It is to make peace with them. My decision to find Dori was an enactment of that gesture. For 40 years I had rejected part of myself, secreted her away from public view so as to hide my shame. Once I bent down to kiss what I thought was my own broken and ugly face, I began to like myself infinitely more. I am no longer that other girl, but I honor her.

An inner radiance began to shine forth, and when I encountered friends I hadn't seen for a while, they would comment on it. "You seem different. What's going on in your life?" It was as though I had hidden in a 40-year-old lizard skin that finally molted. I slid out shimmering green in a dance of delight.

Life is different now. Filled with simple joys, sprinkled with wonder, soaked in grace. There's a knowledge of God's love working in me that I never experienced before. I anticipate each new day and feel God's presence in everything I do. I know I am loved. In fact, He calls me His *beloved.* I experience an intimacy with God I only longed for earlier in life.

In her book *The Dance—Moving to the Rhythms of Your True Self,* Oriah Mountain Dreamer asks a question, the answer to which sums up everything there is to say about authenticity: "What if the question is not why am I so infrequently the person I really want to be, but why do I so infrequently want to be the person I really am?"[26]

CHAPTER 8

PAUSING BY QUIET WATERS
Developing the Practice of Reflection

*The most important reason for keeping a journal is that
every now and then God shows up.*
—Ken Gire, *The Reflective Life*[27]

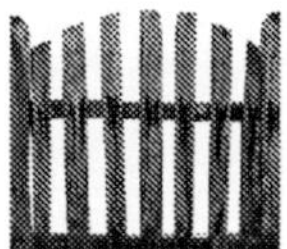

*But I have stilled and quieted myself,
just as a small child is quiet with its mother.*
—Psalm 131:2, NLT

Our journey to the life we want to live inside, the one to which Jesus beckons us, has taken us across thresholds, through doorways, and along passages that require us to wriggle past constricted gates. We've been moving most of that time, but the path turns aside now into a narrow lane and we see ahead a quiet pool with a wooden bench set back from the edge. It's time to sit down and be still; to see if there might be something we need to learn here before we continue on our pilgrimage.

Our culture doesn't put high value on the practice of silence and reflection. Cell phones, iPods, and surround-sound home entertainment systems place silence at a premium. The practice of solitude and quiet is valuable because it provides direction. It empowers us to connect with the undercurrent and to experience oneness with Christ. We can use it to carve out a place in our spirit where we are most receptive to impressions from the Holy Spirit.

For too long, modern Christianity has feared terms such as "hearing from God" or "listening to the Spirit," yet the Bible is replete with references that tell us "My sheep hear my voice" (John 10:27, *NKJV*). What are we afraid of? While there are some who use the phrase "God told me…" to cover their reasons for choices that friends and family have counseled against, we must be careful not to abandon the truth because others have abused it.

The Need to Pause

The idea of the sacred pause is interspersed throughout the Bible. A popular topic in both secular and religious writing today, it remains, however, one of the first things we neglect in our daily routine. At the same time, it's a habit we urgently need to practice with consistence if we hope to connect with God on any level of intimacy.

In the book of Psalms, we find an obscure word, *selah*, that appears over 70 times. While the exact definition of *selah* continues to puzzle scholars, they agree that it most likely means "to pause and consider." Although it is probably a musical notation, it may have been allowed in the text to remind us that stopping to pause and consider is paramount to our journey.

A year ago, I became interested in the Christian Celtic communities of Northumbria (the extreme northeast of England), Scotland, Ireland, and Wales. Like the geography of these regions, Celtic spirituality is rugged, drawing strength from a mystical history. One of these Celtic prayers has become the position from which I begin my own daily ceremony of stillness: "Be still and aware of God's presence within and all around." It helps me quiet myself before God.

God knows us inside and out, having formed us in our mother's womb. His invitation to "be still, and know that I am God" (Psalm 46:10) is a deeply beneficial practice. It is a summons for us to pause in His presence. We do the scripture no harm by rewording it to say, "Be still and know that I AM." Whatever you happen to need today, you can fill in the blank: I AM your *peace*; I AM your *provision*; I AM your *patience*.

"Be still" is translated from Hebrew to mean "to relax, to sink down, to let drop, to be quiet." The Bible draws a word picture in this verse that leads us to the place where we can drop into quietness, where we can relax from the tension of our journey. It's the same familiar words of Psalm 23: "He leads me beside the still waters" (v. 3, *NKJV*).

A Ritual for Stillness

There are appropriate ways to listen to God—ways that are proven and validated by Scripture. Reflection, meditation, and the practice of contemplation, to name only three, are invaluable for those who desire an intimate relationship with Christ.

"How can I learn to practice this?" It's the cry of our hearts. While there are many ways to practice pausing, we come into our own ritual for stillness as we experiment with a variety of practices that promote quiet reflection. After all, we are seekers, and those who seek will find. The methods proposed in this chapter are suggestions to lead you toward a practice of being still.

One of the easiest ways to begin this quest is to find a quiet place and light a candle. Staring at the fire as it dances along the edge of the wick feels like "wrapping the soul around some little flame of hope that God has ignited," as Sue Monk Kidd says in *When the Heart Waits*. Kidd describes our wait as a posture of the spirit: "It's curling up in fogged spaces of the listening heart, sinking into solitude, wrapping the soul around some little flame of hope that God has ignited. It's sitting on the window sill of the heart, still and watching."[28] This is a stunning description of Psalm 46:10.

There are mornings when I walk out on my back porch and hold up my mug of coffee, fresh-brewed and hot, a symbol of the new day. Then I pour out the first sip as an oblation to the Lord, an offering to say, "I give You my heart, all that I am and have. Do as You wish with me this day." I watch the dark liquid soak into the ground and sense that God smiles, perhaps at my foolishness. Still, I think He is pleased. It's one of the ways I practice being quietly aware of His presence all around.

I've always felt at home in the woods. In that realm of half-green light, the anticipation of discovering a hidden mystery compels me to stillness. It's a place where I feel safe and at ease with solitude; a place where I can listen to my life and what it's trying to tell me.

The summer I was nine and my sister, Cheree, was seven, we made what we called "the hideout." The hideout was located in a corner of our backyard under some tall trees and between the narrow space of a double hedge. Constructing it consisted simply of raking away dead leaves and sticks to expose the smooth dirt underneath. Rocks already divided our side yard from the neighbor's, so we used them to form our boundaries. With this minimal preparation, we took the ordinary and made it into a special place where we could hide from the summer sun in cool green shade as we lay on our backs and let the sunlight fall golden and dappled through the canopy of trees onto our faces. I spent hours out there reading books, nibbling on snacks I snuck out of the kitchen, relishing my solitude.

I didn't remember our hideout until one morning recently when I was studying Psalm 91. As I read verse 1, the still and green memory came drifting back unsolicited: "He who dwells in the shelter of the Most High will abide in the shadow of the Almighty" (*NASB*). The shelter, the secret place—a secluded site to gather my thoughts and be still.

Recently on a trip to northern California, I visited a redwood forest. It was my second trip there in a year, and this time I was with a group of curious friends who wanted to know all the details on each marker—how old the trees are, the history of the area, the types of vegetation. As we entered the forest, a hush fell and the air hung with a blue-green mist that enveloped us in its coolness. The farther we walked, the more I wanted to slip away and lose myself in a faery ring—a tight circle of redwoods that form a secret space said to contain magic. The magic for me was the sense of God's presence, His glorious beauty revealed in the forest, the majesty of His creation. I have no trouble being still in such a place.

These examples are simple ways to practice a greater awareness of God's presence with us. Although He invites us to experiment with different locations and traditions to broaden our alertness and instructs us to carve out time alone, we don't always have to be in a cloistered place to experience God. He's there in the ordinary parts of our day. Frederick Buechner points to this truth in *Sacred Journey*:

> There is no chance thing through which God cannot speak—even the walk from the house to the garage that you have walked ten thousand times before, even the moments when you cannot believe there is a God who speaks at all anywhere. He speaks, I believe, and the words he speaks are incarnate in the flesh and blood of our selves and of our own footsore and sacred journeys. [29]

The point of all this is to be still and listen. To pay attention. In order to develop a rhythm, try all the suggestions that follow. Ask God how to wait before Him. Talk to friends about how they quiet their souls. Eventually, your personal style will emerge.

The Gateway to a Reflective Life

Our purpose here is to give simple instruction on the practice of silence. It has many traditions and names: centering prayer, contemplative prayer, practice of stillness, silent mediation. It is practiced by virtually every religion in the world. Most of us have been taught that prayer must utilize words; it must be spoken, whether silently in our minds, or verbally so others might hear. This is just not so. Sometimes prayer is a groaning "which cannot be uttered" (Romans 8:26, *NKJV*).

Learning to wait before God in silence is described in the psalms repeatedly. My favorite, the one that goes straight to my heart, is found in Psalm 131:2:

> But I have stilled and quieted myself,
> just as a small child is quiet with its mother.
> Yes, like a small child is my soul within me (*NLT*).

What I love about this verse is that it teaches me that I can still and quiet my own soul. A "weaned child," it says in the King James Version. A child that's still nursing is fretful and squirming. She demands that her need be met. However, a weaned child has matured to the point that she can wait. She's learned how to quiet herself. This stillness is a resource that enables us to live a centered, peaceful, healthy, sane life. Without it, we will never hear the "still, small voice" of the Lord. We will forfeit the inner guidance that comes from reading God's Word and listening for His directives. We require both sources—the written Word and the spoken word—in order to know what to do and what not to do. They must agree, of course, and where they don't, for people of faith the Word of God is always the final word. Our safety lies solidly in that.

We shouldn't abandon the practice of listening for God's instruction directly, however, because we fear being in error. If we don't have enough faith to believe in Jesus' ability to lead us, our faith is indeed small.

Exercise #1—A Simple Practice of Stillness

Begin this exercise by turning off all electronic sounds that might distract you. Find a comfortable, quiet place to sit. You may want to sit upright in a chair with arms or lay on the floor—facing up as a symbol of receptiveness, facing down as a sign of abandonment. You may enjoy lighting a candle as a signal to your mind and body that you are shifting gears into your practice of stillness.

Sit or lie for whatever length of time it takes you to "center" yourself—in other words, as long as it takes you to let go of worrisome thoughts, your to-do list, or anything else you feel you *should* be doing. The blame voice will tell you this is a waste of your precious time and make various other nagging remarks to prevent you from this practice. It is here you must "quiet yourself as a weaned child" by speaking to the Lord. Something like this, in your own words, will suffice: "Lord Jesus, here I am. I've come to be with You, to spend time in Your presence and to listen to anything You might want to tell me today." It's good to remind yourself that this is not an ordinary prayer time when you come with a list of petitions. That is a different type of prayer, for another time. You are not asking for anything in particular. You are just waiting and listening.

As distractions come (and they will), picture them as boats sailing down the river. You might notice them as they pass, but you do not try to figure out what's on board or where they're headed. If you lit a candle, focus on the candle's flame to keep you centered, or just focus on thoughts of God's love and His kindness toward you. Be at peace, open to God and in listening mode. It will take weeks of practice for you to do this for even five minutes—that is why it is called a "spiritual discipline." You may not feel, see, or hear anything noteworthy at first, but if you continue practicing, in time God will reveal Himself to you in ways you've never before known. He is overjoyed when you give Him this time.

Exercise #2—Using the Scripture for Reflective Reading

For this exercise, first choose a Scripture verse on which you would like to reflect. It should not be longer than a paragraph or two. Next, seated in a comfortable place with your Bible before you, take some time to still your thoughts. Fold in the wings of your intellect by concentrating on your breathing. Breathe in on five counts and release your breath on five counts. Do this at least five times to direct your focus toward the Spirit. The word most often used in the Bible for "spirit" is *breath*. Breath is life; spirit is life. When we die, we have no more breath. Imagine yourself drawing life from God with every inhale and releasing fear, anger, or anxiety with every exhale.

When you feel at peace, open your Bible to the short passage you chose beforehand. Read it over slowly three times. Let yourself be drawn into the words. If it's a scene, imagine yourself there as a bystander or as the person to whom Jesus is speaking. If a phrase or a word seems to attract your attention, think about that word, turning it over in your mind, examining it in depth. Then ask the Lord what He wants you to see in the words. Does He want you to respond with some action? Or is He correcting you? Is this a promise He wants you to believe? Use the words to draw you to Christ—His ways, His love, His teaching, His correction.

After you sense that everything is completed, thank Christ for being with you and showing you these things. Ask His help in putting them into your life this day. This is meditation.

Bungee Jumping for the Brain

There are two components to a reflective life. We have looked at one of them in the gateway to stillness and meditation. The other is to record your life through journaling. As in the practice of stillness, you can design journaling to best fit your needs, personality, and understanding of Scripture on the subject. One component of reflection is accomplished by contemplative prayer; the other is accomplished by drawing a map through journaling. Both practices lead to the same center.

The urge to write down our journey is universal. Of all the ways to pause and consider how we might read the present moment, reflective writing seems among the most effective. It leaves a trail to mark our way, a path to which we can return when lost. Journaling gives our souls time to rest; it lets us sift through the clutter and noise of everyday life. Journal-keeping provides focus, clarity, and balance to issues, concerns and conflicts. The exercise of consistent, life-based writing is like bungee jumping for the brain—it challenges, stretches, and exhilarates. Journaling is a proven way to change, heal, and grow and is the choice of many for deeper spiritual formation.

Keeping a journal requires no special talent, skill, or experience, and it can be lots of fun. There, on a clean white page, we can pour out all the questions, joys, and doubts of our lives. There's no one to judge or criticize our feelings. We are safe from the pointing fingers and wagging tongues. It's our chance to "see" what's going on in our lives.

It's possible that fear hinders some of us from processing our feelings on paper. We are afraid someone will read what we've written and use it against us. Nonetheless, once we determine that journaling is a valid route to a practice of quietness, we do well to take courage and press forward. Here are a few ways to overcome the fear:

- Hide the journal in a secret place
- Keep it in a locked box
- Write in a computer and use a password
- Trust that if the journal is read, the end of the world will not occur

Fran shares the following experience about how she has used journaling in her life:

When I realized the significance of journaling and how important it could be in helping me define my life, my writing at once became stilted and obligatory. The spontaneity I'd enjoyed as a child disappeared in my adult writing. I was trying to journal "properly," whatever that meant. As a young girl, I slept with a notebook and pencil beside my pillow, reasoning that if a great thought or unforgettable dream should invade my sleeping hours, I would be ready to record it. I jotted down my thoughts on different topics, snippets of sweet talk between my sister and her boyfriend, and most of all, the imaginations that filled my waking hours.

As I researched more on the subject of journal writing, I learned that I could return to the joy of recording my thoughts and observations. I determined to put away the rules and regulations and color outside the lines. From now on, my writing would please only me; it was for my eyes only.

Today, my journaling remains unorthodox. I jot down thoughts from a memorable luncheon with my sisters, an afternoon at the lake with grandchildren, or a weekend at the island with friends. I sometimes add jokes, or little drawings, or even a recipe or two. A description of the sky and clouds, the smell of morning, the silken skin of my four-year-old grandson, and my husband's touch are all recorded. I do not write every day, and my entries include a variety of other objects such as photos, cards, articles, and quotes. The pretension is gone. A journal is certainly one place I can just be myself.

Establish Your Style

One of the best parts of this adventure is deciding how, what, where and when you will journal. To set yourself on the course, you may want to first answer some pertinent questions, such as:

- Will you write by hand or use a computer?
- Do you want a bound journal or a loose-leaf notebook?
- Do you prefer writing in an artist's sketchbook without lines, or are lines a must for you?

Once you've decided what you'll use to record your journey, it's time for the fun. The following tips are meant to excavate your creative flow, so let 'er rip. Try as many as strike your fancy and come up with a few of your own.

- Splurge on special pens—go to an art supply story and try them out.
- Write in different colors.
- If you are talented enough to draw, add artwork to your writing.
- If you can't draw, cut pictures from magazines that express your feelings and style or that comprise your wish list.
- Buy a handcrafted leather cover that allows you to add new fillers each year (see oberondesign.com).
- Check out the new fun spiral notebooks when back-to-school supplies come out.
- Paste in cards from friends that you can't bear to throw away.
- Use acid-free glue to affix favorite photos, and then write your comments to the side or even all around the photo.

Next, designate a place to journal. Southwest Florida is notoriously hot and muggy about six months out of the year, so writing outside is a challenge. On cooler days, though, I love to sit on my back porch to write. I feel more alive and part of the universe when I'm in touch with nature (probably a carry-over from those days in the hideout). It helps calm my frenzied thoughts to be among the birds and trees to do my writing. When I'm not outside, I'm nestled in "my corner"—a comfortable chair in my writing studio with a footstool, a good reading light, and a container of pens and markers in every size, color, and shape. There's usually a cup of fresh-brewed coffee or Earl Grey tea to complete the setting. Am I pampering myself? You bet. Life is difficult, and this is one way I extricate myself from the dismal swamp of pressing circumstances, worries, and fears. Any spot will serve the purpose as long there's a bit of privacy and my tools of the trade.

We integrate journaling into our lives by practicing a discipline that suits our goals, temperament, and life circumstances. Different styles of journals aid us in our discipline: dated diaries, sketchbooks or regular journals. Most bookstores carry a large selection of journals. While the word "journal" comes from a French root word that means "daily," it is that menacing word that looms before some of us. We suppose that deciding to journal means we must write volumes in our book and that we must write every day. I love Christina Baldwin's rules for journal writing: (1) date your entries as you go, and (2) don't make any other rules.[30]

If you are a regimented person who feels guilty if you don't write daily, don't buy a dated journal. Look at it this way: if you write once a week, you will have made 52 journal entries in a year. Even if you only make 12, you are recording what's happening in your life and your response to it. These are markers and signposts along the road of life that can provide direction for you and possibly leave a legacy for others. Sometimes, just putting your thoughts down on paper, closing the book and walking away is enough to free your heart to listen more intently to the whispers of God.

A journal records a spiritual quest by uncovering heart truths—by expressing emotion, recording memories or navigating challenges and life passages. I agree with my author friend Janice Elsheimer in her book *The Creative Call*: "Sitting quietly, making time for ourselves alone, pouring out our joy and our sorrow onto the blank pages can be a form of therapy, a gift to ourselves—the gift of simply 'being.'"[31]

Journal writing should be viewed as a process rather than a product. It's a way to explore—not merely to communicate—what we already know and also to uncover new thoughts and ideas, to write down the imaginations of our soul. It is a tool for building a relationship with ourselves.

The purpose of keeping a journal is to help us *see* what we look at. In the back of my journal, I keep a list of all the books I read in a year. I do the same with movies. During the last week of every year, when I hibernate to evaluate my spiritual journey and seek direction for the coming year, I often see how God directed my thinking and actions through those books and movies. It keeps me more aware of His presence within and all around. They may have seemed like random choices to me at the time, but often they turned out to be messages from God. If we pay close enough attention, we can see His footprints buried in the path we've followed, leading us on a trail of new discoveries.

I was thumbing through my old journals recently and came across these words I wrote after I had crossed the rope bridge (see chapter 1) and resigned my position to write and speak full time:

Thursday, June 9, 2005

Only a few more steps and I'll be there. The bridge isn't swinging anymore. I look ahead to the other side and see the woods, tall pines, peppered with spruce and cedar. The underbrush is light and the floor of the forest is carpeted with a thick blanket of pine needles. My eyes are drawn to a slight movement at the edge of the trees, and all of a sudden He steps out grinning. He waves at me. "You made it," He says.

If I had not picked up my journal to jot down my thoughts that morning, I would never have seen that picture in my mind's eye. It just came as I wrote, not preconceived in any way on my part. It makes me laugh and cry still—every time I read it—to know that God does lead me and at times gives specific instructions. The best part, however, is knowing He is with me. He assures me, in His own distinctive way, that I have heard His voice.

Record a Threshold or a Passage

Specific seasons in our lives deserve particular noting: a last child leaves home, our hair turns gray, a parent faces illness or death, we suffer a bout with breast cancer, we take a trip to Italy, our family homestead is sold, we leave a failed marriage. These are trails we blaze, passages of life worth recording.

A year into my daughter Texas's fight with cocaine addiction, I chose to record what was happening. I bought a small, red journal with

Teddy bears on it. At 17, she still seemed a child, but she was leaving her childhood behind. I understand now that the journal cover was my way of trying to hold on to my little girl. Just the act of choosing the book, running my finger over the cover, feeling our loss, was my way of facing the truth. Eventually, I wrote page after page about my sadness, my fear for her safety, my tenuous hope for her future. This helped me realize I was living this story. It had a beginning, a middle, and would one day have an end, even if it wasn't the end I had hoped for.

The passage you record need not be a painful one. It doesn't even need to be significant at first glance. Any journey, whether inner or outer, can provide abundant material. You can make a gratitude journal, a vacation journal, or a journal in which you write to or about a particular person—such as one that records a legacy for a grandchild, as Fran does. You can write a letter you'll never mail to clear the air or to get something off your chest.

Passage journals can be written months, or even years, after the external passage is completed. In this case, the reflection itself becomes the event, the passage through which you are moving. Often, if the event you're writing about is extremely traumatic or painful, as in the death of a child, it may be years before you can see clearly enough to write about it.

Whether you are writing about a passage that's occurring now or are attempting to understand something that has already occurred, the course of action is the same: begin as soon as you feel the urge to write. Write often and from the deepest part of your heart until you've passed through the story and stand at the threshold of a new experience. The story doesn't have to have a firm ending in order for you to close the book.

Writing Your Emotions

Handling our emotions is vital to a journey toward significance. To write about anger, for instance, we must hurdle what we've been taught both by our parents and the Church—that feelings are sinful and the mark of immaturity. To be sure, we cannot be pouty little girls who stamp their feet whenever they don't get their way. Yet all anger is not sin. God makes provision for our natural anger by teaching us how to be angry in a constructive way (see Ephesians 4:26).

"How do we do that?" you may ask. To admit anger over circumstances or injustice is an honest, human response. Hiding that we're angry is a sin because it's lying or, at best, pretending to be "okay" when we're not. God Himself gets angry, but He does not sin. Holding on to our anger, petting and coddling it, *is* sin, but there are healthy ways to process it.

In this excerpt from a friend's letter, she states with frankness how important it is to be honest about our feelings when we talk to God:

The single most important thing I've learned over the years is that communication is the key to every relationship—and that includes our relationship with the Lord. Even during my darkest, most despondent times, I try not to lose touch with talking to the Lord. It might only be shaking my fist at Him, yelling at Him and asking just what in the blankety-blank He is doing, but *that* is communication. I mean, the Lord already knows I'm angry and upset, right? So what's the use in approaching His throne with blessings when what I feel in my heart is a cursing? I have let it fly more than once. And you know what? He still takes me on His lap, holds me and tells me He understands. The minute I yell at Him and let my feelings be known, He is right there soothing my wounds. I feel ashamed, of course, but somehow cleansed. He has really big shoulders, and I have leaned on them more times that I can count.

A journal can serve as the emotional dumping ground of the soul. Here is a safe place to vent, to pour out the torment and doubt, to ask the questions that beg asking until we empty the garbage. The same exercise helps us process fear and anxious thoughts. King David was a master at this. Listen to the questioning and grief expressed in these words from Psalm 42:9:

> Sometimes I ask God, my rock-solid God,
> "Why did you let me down?
> Why am I walking around in tears,
> harassed by enemies?" (*THE MESSAGE*).

David goes on to question himself and ask why he is so down in the dumps. By the end of his venting spell, he usually comes back to the reality that his only hope is in God, who listens and acts according to His own purposes. This is an effective journaling practice, and applying it can sometimes save the cost of therapists and counselors. Stuffing our anger, fear, and frustration only leads to hopelessness and depression.

Journaling as Play

When journaling becomes something added to an already over-worked to-do list, it's time to change your attitude about its purpose and merits. Make journal writing child's play (see the previous list for artistic suggestions). After all, it's for your eyes only. Doodle in the margins. Write silly stories about red-eyed lizards or talking rabbits. Amuse yourself with sketches or cut out magazine pictures and paste them in your journal. It's good mental and spiritual exercise to stretch your imagination. If you are a writer, play with the sounds of words and keep a "favorite words" list. Do a timed writing during which you write whatever comes to mind for 10 minutes. Sometimes the greatest gift you can give yourself is to lighten up and *not* deal with the frightening questions.

A few years back when I was deciding to make writing my career, I happened upon a writing exercise that became a breakthrough for me. I was reading Janice Elsheimer's book *The Creative Call,* in which she challenges her readers to write three pages every morning for the purpose of developing free-flow writing. This type of writing is spontaneous and even nonsensical. The purpose is to move your pen over the paper and write whatever comes to mind.

One morning as I dutifully scripted my "morning pages," as Janice calls them, I began to journal on this thought: *Why I refuse to write.* I decided to see if I could get in touch with my subconscious thoughts and let them rise to the surface of my intellect. I gave this part of myself the name "Evening Star." Here's what came forth:

> Evening Star is a playful and creative side of me. She is also shy and doesn't like demanding control freaks who set goals to stimulate her to get to work. She will only come out where there is freedom to dance and sing and twirl about in her writing. She's still trying to find out what she likes best—prose, fiction or just plain journaling. Be nice to Evening Star and respect her idiosyncrasies. She's a bit temperamental and needs time to warm up before you put her in the Boston Marathon. She's full of ideas, you know, and when the pressure is off and she's allowed to play, wonderful sentences bubble up and flow out from the tip of her pen point.

"Evening Star" was my self-designated Indian name as a child. (I always wanted to be an Indian.) When I thought about my playful side, I discovered she was still there, even though I hadn't thought of those childhood games in years.

I must admit I am fearful you will think I've got a loose screw somewhere after you read those two paragraphs. Yet I'll take the risk if it means you'll understand that writing can be a lot of fun. I learned things that day about my writing self that I never knew. They serve me well now that I'm writing all the time. Journaling for play often turns into a peek behind the curtain of our souls. It is well worth the time and space we create for it.

Writing Your Prayers

A worthy practice in journal keeping is to write out our prayers. Much of my journal writing has turned out to be expressions of my deepest longings, fears, hopes, expectations, and dreams written out to God, my Father. The journal writing becomes an open dialogue between us.

Like David, I've been brutally honest with God. I've written my heart out to Him and come away from the experience lighter, freer, and with a better understanding of where I am. The page simply listens. Ultimately, my Father cares what I think and is represented by those waiting pages. It is a glorious experience to record prayers. With amazement, I have reread prayers I didn't remember writing to discover many of them answered. If I hadn't written them down, I would have missed the blessing of seeing how God worked it all out. Our memory can only carry us so far.

Spiritual writing can consist of a vast array of practices:

- *Writing the Scripture.* This is a method of exploring the meaning in a passage. Write it out in several translations (*NIV, AMP, THE MESSAGE, NJB*) and then dissect what you feel God is saying to you personally through the words and how He wants you to respond to the message.

- *Writing dreams.* Write out the dreams you get in sleep, scoping out what the Spirit of God might be showing you about your life, spiritual problems, or your future.

- *Praying anxieties.* List your fears and anxious thoughts and then take them before the Lord. Ask Him to direct your steps with each one and then cast your cares (unload them) on Him. This kind of purging will leave you peaceful and in tune with what God is doing in your life (see Philippians 4:6).

- *Praying the future.* The Bible tells us that God directs our steps; therefore, we need not fear our future. When we sense we are overly concerned with an area of our future, we can write it out in a journal and tell God we will trust Him with it. It helps us to make a declaration in writing of our trust—a way to let go of control.

Write Your Belief System

One of the easiest ways to begin to journal for the first time is to write out your belief system. Rather than theology, this is a snapshot of the beliefs that reflect your life experience at this point in time. What are your governing values, the things in life you won't compromise? These can be your convictions, principles, even your opinions. Some of your beliefs will have been with you since childhood, while others will be based on recent discoveries about yourself. Set aside a two-hour block of time where you can work uninterrupted. Go to the beach or sit outside on the deck. Curl up on the couch or make your entries electronically. Just do it!

At the top of a clean journal page, write "I believe…" and then list your thoughts. Don't strive or strain, just write until there's nothing left trying to push itself out onto the page. Here are a few examples of questions to jumpstart the project that you can use to jog your creativity (for further examples, check out www.writingthejourney.com, www.lifejournal.com or www.journal.lifetips.com):

- Who is God? What kind of relationship do I have with Him? What kind of relationship do I want to have?
- What do I value most in life? How important are material possessions? Which ones matter the most? Would I be happy if I lost everything I have tomorrow? What possession would I be most upset about losing?
- In the scheme of things, how important is money? Where does my money come from? Where does it go? Do I have enough? What would I do with more? How much would be enough? Am I content?
- Do I take the time to write letters, or would I rather talk on the phone? Do I listen or talk more? Why? What does this say about me?

- Where and what do I consider "home"? What makes it home? Do I nurture myself? Does my home nurture others? Do I have a balance between care-giving and care-receiving? Why?
- Do my feelings make me uncomfortable? Why? Am I able to express my feelings to others? What makes me cry? Do I laugh a lot?
- Where does my personal style show up most (clothing, decorating, cooking, hospitality, children, the arts)? What is my favorite color? What style do I want to be known for?
- What do I want to leave as my legacy to the world? What natural talents and abilities do I have? What skills have I acquired? What spiritual gifts do I possess?
- How do I feel about my body? How is my health? Do I eat healthy foods and get exercise? Why or why not?
- How important are friends in my life? Growing up, did I have a lot of friends, or a few? How do I balance time spent with other people and time spent alone? What happens when I get out of balance? How important are relationships? Am I more comfortable with friends of the same or opposite sex?
- Am I afraid to die? What happens when I do? Where was I before I was born? Do I pray about how I will die and whether I will be prepared? Why not?[32]

You might find it helpful to put this list of questions inside your journal and read through it now and then to see if there's a question that invites your consideration. You may notice new and different opportunities appearing in your life, doors that open to you because you've expressed a desire to know more. Some of these opportunities are sent to test your beliefs. You may be surprised at what you write when you ask yourself these questions. As you search through your belief system, you may decide to let go of old ideas you no longer value. Then you can journal about that!

Hungry for Quietness

Whether we're 25 or 55, single or married, we're somewhere in the middle of a spiritual quest. Even if we are unconscious sojourners, the act of choosing to read a book such as *Thresholds and Passages* reveals we are among those searching for a fuller understanding of life.

Without reflection time to pause, consider, examine and evaluate, life reduces itself to monotony and boredom. The decade of the 1980s was like that for me. My days were boringly predictable. I had four children at home and I went to work, fixed supper, helped with homework, did laundry, fell in bed exhausted, and started the same ritual over again the next day. I didn't journal much in those days.

Then one day, I crossed the street from my office to the bank and something happened that changed everything. As I waited in the teller's line, I noticed a bouquet of flowers at her window. They were ordinary flowers, the kind that grow in abundance in most Florida yards year round. They grew in *my* yard. As I reflected on those flowers, my thoughts went something like this: *I would give anything to have fresh flowers in my house, but I can't afford them. She must have picked them out of her yard. Why can't I pick the ones in my yard?* When I went home that evening, that is just what I did.

If we don't grapple with the questions and learn to ask "What's it all about, Alfie?" the very perfume of our lives evaporates with the ordinariness of it all. That day in the bank, I reclaimed my life. The teller's flowers called me home to myself. Within weeks, I also dug out my old journal and, starting with that story, began to wade through the quagmire of my life. That single act brought me out of my long slumber. Instead of pulling the covers over my head, I decided to come out and feel the heat of the sun once again on my face.

The fog didn't leave immediately. I needed to practice stillness before I could quell the inner chaos. This is when I learned to pause. Sometimes, I just sat still on the shore of the Gulf of Mexico, my arms lashed tight around my knees, wind blowing my hair, the smell of the sea fresh around me. I did it sometimes just to keep from flying apart. In my weekly planner, I penciled in dates with myself, times when I opted for a walk instead of lunch or trotted down to the beach, journal in hand, to record what my life was saying at the moment. Mostly, I just learned to still my soul.

Spiritual questing touches not only the dramatic and spectacular moments of life but also every bit of the ordinary. Marking our passage through earth aids us in rising above the haze and the bewildering detours that leave us to spin in confusion. We note where the sacred and the ordinary converge. The writing forms a map—a navigation tool—that illuminates our path. Keeping a journal can symbolize an open acceptance of the life we've been handed; a positive way of acknowledging that it is valid and worthy to record.

My journal accepts me just as I am—the same way God accepts me. Like a loving and faithful friend, it is constant, ready to receive my whining and sniveling as well as my joy and gratitude. It neither judges nor scolds. It just listens with infinite patience as I pour out the wheat and chaff together. Then it helps me sift through the whole, throw away the chaff, and keep the good wheat that's left. It's my personal travelogue—a triptych of my journey.

More Threshold Work

Scripture abounds with rich symbolism that depicts our passage from the profane to the sacred. This ability to separate the precious from the worthless is a skill that must be learned and developed. It is depicted for us in the story of Jacob at Bethel.

In this story, Jacob is fleeing his home, having stolen the birthright from his brother, Esau. On his way, he spends the night in a lonely place. As he sleeps with a stone—which symbolizes an altar—for a pillow, he has a dream in which a ladder appears. The ladder is an instrument of passage, a place of transition, an object that can take us up or down. In his dream, he sees angels going up and coming down the ladder. At the top, the Lord appears to him and instructs him in regard to his future, his protection, his family, and his purpose. Later, Jacob likens the place to the gate of heaven. He pours oil on the stone and dedicates the place by naming it "Bethel," the house of God. He walks away changed (see Genesis 28:10-20).

Similarly, in the third chapter of Joshua we read the story of young Joshua who is Moses' replacement. The people have finally completed their 40-year wilderness journey and are now preparing to enter a land of promise the Lord gave to them by covenant decades earlier. Joshua will lead them through the Jordan River, a liminal space between the already and the not yet. They are out of Egypt, out of the wilderness, but not yet in the Promised Land. The Lord instructs them to separate themselves, to hallow the moment they are in, all in preparation to cross the threshold. When they complete the mission, they take stones from the river and build a memorial (see Joshua 4:5-8). It is a place where they have met with God.

In the New Testament, Jesus is baptized in that same Jordan River, which represents surrender, death, and abandonment. Immediately, He is led by the Spirit into the wilderness for 40 days of solitude. He is preparing to begin His earthly ministry, and this is the crucible, the place of testing and transition. As with Jesus, this is often where *we* meet the devil face to face; the place where the passageway is blocked. And like Jesus, we have guardians in this place whose assignment is to assist us in crossing the threshold (see Matthew 4:11).

We have noted often that there is threshold work to be done if we hope to seize the true meaning of our lives. Perhaps none of what we've previously suggested comes close to the importance of intentional re-flection—periods of solitude and a place to record what's going on in our lives at the moment.

Too often we have presented ourselves at the end of some church aisle, hoping that a spiritual leader will pray over us to "deliver us from evil." While we do acknowledge that epiphanies, and even some forms of deliverance, can take place in that setting, it does not preclude our necessary threshold work. Here is where we thresh through the grain of our lives, pounding away the husks as we abandon our ways for God's ways and our will for His. It's the place where we let go of damaging emotions to imbibe His sweet peace. First Peter 3:4 reminds us that a gentle and tranquil spirit in the heart of a woman is highly valuable in God's eyes. We just do not gain this without the threshold work. This is holy work, carried out by the Holy Spirit in the sacred ground of our hearts.

NURTURING YOUR NEW LIFE

CHAPTER 9

CALLING THE CIRCLE OF SACRED SISTERHOOD
Choosing Companions for the Journey

And Pooh said to Piglet "Life is so much friendlier with two."
—A.A. Milne, *Winnie the Pooh*

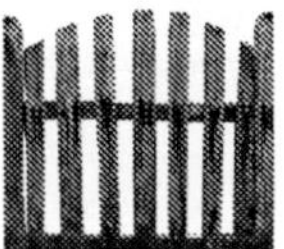

And these God-chosen lives all around—what splendid
friends they make!
—Psalm 16:3, *THE MESSAGE*

There are few things I anticipate more than an afternoon shared with close friends. One time back in junior high, I was rushing through the halls on a hectic afternoon when a friend handed me a crumpled paper with these words: "Oh, the comfort—the inexpressible comfort of feeling safe with a person—having neither to weigh thoughts nor measure words, but pouring them all right out, just as they are, chaff and grain together; certain that a faithful hand will take and sift them, keep what is worth keeping, and then with the breath of kindness blow the rest away."[33] I've been on a quest for that level of friendship ever since.

An Early Start

Squeals of delight pierce the air as two little girls throw their arms around each other, jump up and down, and both talk at the same time. They are best friends, kindred spirits, bosom buddies. How early we start on this path. All of us have participated in this same sweet ritual.

Today, we experience similar but more mature feelings when we greet a friend. Concern may surface as our eyes search her face and pick up an expression clouded with worry. On the other hand, we share her joys with unmasked delight. Tiny hidden antennae pick up key words as our friend shares tidbits of her life. We are tuned in to a secret channel that exists between us, a cord that weaves us together heart to heart.

Fran and I agree that when the two of us meet, words tumble forth and we can't seem to get them out fast enough. Neither age, distance nor time apart seems to matter. Fran says that regardless of whether I've gained 10 pounds since she last saw me, or whether her hair is three shades grayer, we each feel taller, smarter, funnier, and more together than ever when we are in each other's presence. Without skipping a beat, we begin talking right where we left off. Being with my friend is indescribable joy.

"Girlfriends." The word evokes images of young girls whispering their secrets; or two young women, telephones pinned between ear and shoulder, one with a toddler balanced on her hip the other on the couch folding clothes; or two women, shopping bags piled around their feet, relishing an afternoon cup of coffee at an outdoor café. If we are fortunate, the memories that spring to mind are of happy relationships that have enriched our lives.

My first definition of true friendship came when I was eight years old and Mother read these words to me from *Anne of Green Gables:*

"Marilla," she demanded presently, "do you think that I shall ever have a bosom friend in Avonlea?"

"A—a what kind of a friend?"

"A bosom friend—an intimate friend, you know—a really kindred spirit to whom I can confide my inmost soul. I've dreamed of meeting her all my life. I never really supposed I would, but so many of my loveliest dreams have come true all at once that perhaps this one will too. Do you think it's possible?"[34]

The Desire for Sisterhood

The life of lavish abundance that's offered to each of us Christ-followers is meant to be lived alongside companions. While Jesus knew how to draw aside for prayer and quiet reflection, He was rarely alone for long. He was in the Temple teaching, or in the streets healing and blessing, or seated at various dinner gatherings discussing truth about his Father's kingdom, or hanging out with His men. He understood the necessity and comfort of relationship.

Jesus called the 12 men He mentored for three years His friends (see John 15:14-15.) It takes little imagination to picture them being serious, praying together, talking about issues of the day or listening to Him explain a new way of life, but it's a little harder for us to picture them around a campfire laughing, eating, and poking fun at one another as men do. They not only had a working relationship but also enjoyed companionship. Although Jesus knew *them* intimately, *they* struggled to figure out who He was.

In her national bestseller *Jesus CEO,* Laurie Beth Jones talks about Jesus' relationship with His 12 friends. She calls them "staff" because of the title of her book:

Jesus spent lots of time with his staff. And I wonder whether it wasn't really the picnics and the echoes of his laughter that bound their hearts to him so. Because ultimately they moved heaven and earth just to be with him again...that theme of oneness came through right before he died, because perhaps Jesus' real mission was about companionship.[35]

Outside of our family, girlfriends probably have more influence on us than any other relationships. As women we process joys, sorrows, situational dilemmas, fears, stress, and almost everything in between with our girlfriends. They do the same with us. If the friendship is healthy, there's a balance in things we share. When conversations turn out to be negative and needy, it becomes more like counselor and counselee than companionship. If everything is mostly happiness and glee, the relationship lacks authenticity.

After years of trial and error—girlfriends who loved with fierce loyalty, the ravages of betrayal, and unexpected surprises both good and bad—we find ourselves in a green meadow of pure delight, a sacred circle of sisterhood. In our youth, we seldom possess the necessary wisdom to choose our friends well. Hard-learned lessons teach us that nourishing friendships are the result of choice as much as chance.

In his book *The Four Loves,* C.S. Lewis calls friendship the most spiritual of all loves and reminds us that, for the Christian, nothing is by chance. In the parable of the talents, we are given life within certain parameters of God's choice, and within those boundaries He expects us to multiply, or add to, the original deposit (see Matthew 25:15). What if in addition to the abilities, resources, and gifts God gives us, we would also give an account of how we used our friendships? It's a sobering thought—and one worth exploring.

Building Friendships that Enhance

Stable, healthy friendships are mutual—mutual in commitment, honesty, and openness. One time, a friend gave me a beautiful gold pin in the shape of a pitcher. It was studded with tiny rhinestones, and at the lip was a dangling stone that caught the light when it moved. My friend watched me unwrap the package, and as I lifted the pin from the box she said, "This is to remind you that sometimes you're the pitcher and other times you're the cup."

Over the years, we learn that if we are always the pitcher, we'll find ourselves in relationships that, for us, are all give and no take. Something like a revolving door. We find ourselves going nowhere except in circles. Eventually, if we continue to allow the friendship to drain us, we come up depleted. Emotionally bankrupt. My friend, Pat, gave me the pin to remind me that I need to be the cup as much as the pitcher. It's important that we each have friends who pour into us as well as take from us.

If we have to *be* a certain way to sustain a friendship, it's time to decide if we want to keep playing games. When we constantly tiptoe around a certain friend because she is easily offended or too strongly opinionated, we conclude the friendship is no longer working. It becomes more work than we are willing to invest because the labor is one-sided.

The following list is a good starting place for you to use to evaluate your relationships. Imagine for a moment you and your friend together for the afternoon, enjoying one of your favorite activities. Does this friendship:

- Provide support, arms to hold you up when needed?
- Challenge you to raise the bar of your character?
- Provide accountability?
- Involve true commitment?
- Display mutual respect?
- Call you to times of play and celebration?
- Challenge you to grapple with the hard questions?
- Adhere to strict confidentiality?
- Give you new perspective on a personal issue?
- Offer wise and godly counsel without the other person trying to "fix" you?
- Provide a safe place for you to share your heart?

If you can answer yes to most of these questions, the relationship between you and your friend is healthy. In the areas where you have doubts, it might be good to sit down and go over the list together, deciding in which places change is needed.

Destructive Relationships

It's unnerving for us to admit to ourselves that some friendships no longer nurture us or the other person. I took pride in being a faithful friend. If I committed to a friendship, I felt it was my honor and obligation to be there for that person for life. It took a few shattering separations before I could see that some friendships were God's gift for a season. By that, I don't mean they were fair weather friendships, but that God brought certain people into my life for His own purposes. When that purpose had been accomplished, the relationship often came to an end.

One particular friend (I'll call her Marianne) came to me several years before the darkest period of my life. I was so hungry for affirmation and approval during that time that I had unconsciously surrounded myself with needy people. She was a new Christian and eager to serve. With an uncommon gift of perception and discernment, she soon realized I was a near-empty vessel. So she took it upon herself to be the arms that held me up. She loved me, prayed for me, and gave me wise counsel, and I opened to her love like a water-deprived seed. Until then, no one had ever ministered to *me*. I didn't have mutual relationships. I was mostly the pitcher and seldom the cup.

Marianne was as faithful as any friend who ever existed. But after years of standing by me in desperate times, her own spiritual health began to suffer. She realized that the relationship was becoming destructive because I needed more than any one friend could give. I also needed to make changes in my life that were going to involve a process—one that she felt was not her responsibility. Wisely, she just let the friendship die. It took me much longer. I thought of her often and longed for the companionship we'd shared, but over time I was able to let go. The season of our closeness passed.

While we have reconnected, we are now both in different places. She has grown into a lovely, strong Christian leader, and I have come to realize that something I once called loyalty is actually unhealthy codependence. God desires to lead us forward to new and safer places, where His grace enables us to lean on *Him* as the core of our strength.

Destructive relationships also have characteristics. These include:

- Possessive of our time
- Gossipy
- Emotionally draining
- Often the cause of offense
- Boring and predictable
- Not spiritually uplifting
- One-sided

If after reading this you look honestly at your current friendships and can admit that any are destructive, seek a loving way to detach. If you attempt to explain yourself and the other person in the relationship isn't ready to hear, it could be hurtful. Just let go and move on. If the person asks you later what happened, that may be an opportunity to let them know about the change in you rather than speak about the change they need.

King David was wise enough to know he needed to choose his friends. He put it this way: "I'm a friend and companion of all who fear you, of those committed to living by your rules" (Psalm 119:63, *THE MESSAGE*).

Sharpening the Tools

Have you ever tried to peel an apple with a dull kitchen knife? It's maddening at best and, if you're like me, you never learned how to sharpen a knife. As Fran and I worked on our ideas for conferences and this book, our friendship was tested. Our first few years as "just friends" were filled with laughter, prayer for our families, trips to a nearby tropical island with other friends, excursions to my house at the lake with our husbands, and a level of friendship that was comfortable and easy. We basked in the ambient light of our common interests.

However, the more we worked on writing our journey and attempted to translate our experiences into a path others could follow, the more our differences began to surface. At first we were dismayed. *What's happening to our friendship?* Neither of us talked about it, but as the haze of separation settled like a deep blue fog we knew it was time to address our feelings.

We met one night to talk, cry, and pray. Our task had become hard work with little joy because we were working with dull tools. Ecclesiastes says it with such simple words: "Since a dull ax requires great strength, sharpen the blade. That's the value of wisdom; it helps you succeed" (10:10, *NLT*).

Relationships are great levelers. Whether between a couple in marriage, a parent and child, or between friends, attempting to live in sync brings with it the awareness of not only our individual strengths but also the reality of our faults and weaknesses. Unless we can extend grace to each other, the trip will be rough, causing not only motion sickness but also sickness of heart.

It took time, but Fran and I eventually saw that God was putting us in juxtaposition in order to sharpen us, to use our friendship and working relationship like fine sandpaper to rub off the places that kept us from working with sharpness and acuity. As we allowed Him to do the work required, we were able to use our combined gifts to cut to the core of important issues in the lives of the women to whom He sent us. The words of Proverbs 27:17 became precious and life giving to us: "You use steel to sharpen steel, and one friend sharpens another" (*THE MESSAGE*).

After sharpening a tool or knife, it should be carefully cleaned and oiled before use. God's love for Fran and I cleansed us from our months of frustration and renewed our love for each other. If faith and trust are the foundation of taking a journey with Christ, love is the garment we must wear to endure the arduous trek. It protects us from all the devices of our enemy and from the elements of the world that would incapacitate us in our work. Without love—both for Jesus and for each other—we fail in carrying out the most important of all assignments He gives.

Friends on Purpose

It is not selfish to decide to move on to new relationships that mutually enhance each person in it—in fact, it is wise. Proverbs has much to say about destructive friendships, while on the other hand the writer reminds us that the person "who covers over an offense promotes love" (Proverbs 17:9, *NIV*). Life is too short to spend emotional energy and commitment on people who do not want a life of joy, peace, and unselfish love. We aren't on equal ground. The values that govern our actions are different. There will be conflict about even the most basic issues.

When two acquaintances share their thoughts about family, books, current events, beliefs, or recipes, what often sparks a new friendship is a mutual opinion or interest. "You like that too? I thought I was the only one who felt that way!" In a flash, a tiny cord of respect forms. When pursued, it will usually uncover other mutual attractions.

Jesus was committed to those He called. He "called to Him those He Himself wanted. And they came to Him" (Mark 3:13-21, *NKJV*). His choice had nothing to do with selfishness and everything to do with purpose. Once we've responded to God's call to live our lives according to His purpose, He establishes our course. It's healthy and valuable to ascertain how our current friendships measure up to His standard. As followers of Christ, we ultimately understand that nothing in our lives is by chance. "You did not choose Me, but I chose you" (John 15:16, *NKJV*). God brings people into our lives who will assist us in carrying out His purpose. Some are teachers or mentors, some acquaintances and companions. Only a few are part of that inner circle reserved to spiritual sisterhood.

A Sacred Sisterhood

Whether we call our intimate friends our sisters, Ya-Yas, or girl-friends, they are a rich source of joy and blessing. One of our friends has a group called GNOs—Girls Night Out.

Along the road, we've discovered it is impossible to be intimate with 12 girlfriends. Even Jesus had an inner circle of three, and yet the group wasn't a clique. Onlookers may call it that or a "mutual admiration society," and we may hear the voice of envy. When others who long for their own meaningful relationships watch us from afar, criticism rises. It's not logistically possible, however, to interact on a deep level with more than three or four people.

It's not as though we go out and select three people to be our inner circle. While it may appear that Jesus chose His inner circle, it is more likely that they just emerged from the larger group as those His Father selected. In the same way, the Holy Spirit will reveal that sacred circle to us. It may take some time—even years—for it all to come together, but when it does, it's a priceless treasure. Having three friends who are willing to commit to the values mentioned above deeply changes the way we live our lives. We decide to pay the price to be there for one another. We don't take each other for granted.

Fran tells of the time she awakened to the truth that friendship as a sacred sisterhood would only come with a price:

The dim lights in the waiting room added to the somberness as Kathryn and I spoke with hushed voices. Our eyes burned from lack of sleep, yet we continued to talk, reluctant to be the first one to fall asleep. We had kept vigil all day between the waiting room and Mark's ICU room where we tiptoed from time to time to check his breathing. Mark had been in and out of the hospital many times, but I sat with my friend because I loved her. Our watch that night was not very different from many other times during Mark's long illness that we stood side by side, huddled together in the emergency room or at his bedside. Investing this time into our relationship was not something

I had bargained for. No one told me it would be part and parcel of being Kathryn's friend. I embraced the fun times—shopping, lunches, parties—happy moments when we enjoyed a cup of tea, laughing over silly things. This was the bare bones of a friendship no one had ever discussed with me.

Only in my thirties, I faced a level of friendship beyond anything I'd embraced to that point. This wasn't just a tea party. My heart told me this was the test of sisterhood—to wade into the deep water and feel the icy grip of questions that have no answers. I saw raw fear on her face, and though I often wanted to bolt for home and pretend this wasn't real, I was in for the long haul. When Mark did die years later, Kathryn lived in California and I lived in Florida. His body was flown to Wisconsin, and Bill and I flew up for the funeral. Friends now for more than 35 years, we've made generous deposits into each other's emotional bank accounts. We love to spend the profits of our investment each time we get together, though we have to travel half a continent to get to each other.

Friends are teachers of our hearts. By interacting with them, we learn to let go of grudges, resentments, and envious thoughts. We face fears—both ours and theirs—and learn how to accept loss together. In the process, we release unrealistic ideals by the practice of love and wisdom rather than criticism and isolation.

Allow the Circle to Emerge

Because true friends are so essential for our journey, it is right for us to pray for the right ones. When we entrust God with the right to choose our friends, many delightful surprises result.

When Fran and I came together with our sacred sisterhood, it was because we planned it. We established our own preferences, we discussed needs and desires, and we took months to share our life stories with each other. It seemed right to know our histories—the good, the bad, and the stuff in between. Later, we decided that when we have serious gatherings (all our gatherings are not serious), each person brings something tangible that is symbolic of where she is at the moment.

One time, our friend Erma brought a ball comprised of dead vines wrapped together. She explained that at the moment she felt as dry and fragile as those vines and that she could easily break should even one piece of her soul be touched in the wrong way.

Sometimes, the objects we bring depict an understanding we've recently discovered, or maybe an object from a recent trip. We find this keeps us focused on the purpose of our friendship: *a circle of friends first committed to Jesus Christ; committed to each other in the areas of listening, praying and supporting; and committed to the joyful prospects of whatever lies ahead.* That defines our mission. Our pledge to one another is a reflection of that mission:

- To do whatever it takes to spur each other on to Christlikeness.
- To choose life in all its magnificent splendor.
- To be authentic and honest with each other.
- To rely on the Holy Spirit for our direction.
- To be there for one another—no matter what!

This sacred sisterhood can be a group that enjoys special meals, travels to interesting places, invests time in mission projects, plays together, has once-a-year retreats, or establishes ceremonies of remembrance that have unique meaning only to those in the group. You will want to share Scripture and pray together. Sometimes, you'll just cry with each other.

In her book *The Mermaid Chair*, Sue Monk Kidd describes an unspoken bond that exists between the mother of a woman named Jessie and her two friends. They are in their sixties now, and while Jessie has known them since she was a girl, she's evaluating them at this point in time as an empty, lonely woman. As the four women go to the beach one night to relive the "all girls picnic," Jessie sees their relationship with new eyes. "I'd never done any of those things my mother had done. Never danced on a beach. Never made a bonfire. Never waded into the ocean at night with laughing women and tied my life to theirs."[36]

Do those words call to you? Are you longing for friendships like this? They are out there for *us* real live women, not only for women in novels. The first step is always desire. It's good to long for relationships that are mutually enriching. The longing is the beginning of a prayer. Go ahead and pray it.

Our Own Friendship

As I related earlier, the first thing I ever noticed about Fran Lankford was her gorgeous silver hair. My own hair is color-treated, as close to the original as my age allows. I felt envious of anyone who had the courage to let her true colors show through with such a stunning result. She tempts me to let my hair go grey, if for no other reason than for someone to say, "Sail on, silver girls."

Fran is a constant reminder of how much fun life should be. After years of working in the hospital and hearing women on their deathbeds lament about all they missed, she has a personal agenda to wring out of life every pleasure and joy available to her. For instance, on a recent trip we made together with our other Ya-Yas to visit Dori, she insisted on picking up Gladys, Dori's Indian Runner duck. The duck was captivating, I must admit, looking something like a bowling pin on feet. Within seconds of picking it up, however, Fran had a dark brown spot running down her lime green shirt. She couldn't care less. She wanted a picture of herself with that duck.

I'm more the contemplative sort, who if left to herself for 10 minutes will most likely end up at someone's bookshelf thumbing through chapters of a book, looking for who knows what. This irritates Fran no end, as she believes it is right and proper to be in the conversational flow at all times. She's called me to task several times for this. I do try to comply, but if the conversation lags or too many are competing to be heard in it, I'm likely to wander off. Fran's learned to deal with it. Being with her has refined my table manners, taught me to pay more attention to the present moment, and helped me practice forgiveness.

Not that she's all play. We've had a number of serious moments: accompanying a younger friend to court to help her regain custody of her daughter, standing by a Ya-Ya as she endured the shock and pain of divorce, supporting parents who found out a child was using drugs.

We are partners in ministry and play. We are blessed that our husbands are close friends as well, and we often talk of the four of us taking a trip to Italy. In our travels around the United States speaking and ministering, we've come to understand the ebb and flow of our friendship. Fran has affirmed and blessed me countless times. As I watch her function in her spiritual gifts and natural talents, I see how we have different strengths and weaknesses.

A good friendship is something like a marriage. In his wisdom, King Solomon had this to say about friends: "You are better off to have a friend than to be all alone, because then you will get more enjoyment out of what you earn. If you fall, your friend can help you up. But if you fall without having a friend nearby, you are really in trouble" (Ecclesiastes 4:9-11, *CEV*). When I am in trouble, Fran is there to help. She is my kindred spirit.

Fran responds on how she sees our friendship:

She caught my eye right away, tall and well dressed. My kind of girl. I was new to her church when I saw the announcement of her upcoming ordination. I wondered if anyone had volunteered to have the reception. Hardly knowing Cathee, I nevertheless gladly took on the project of celebrating and honoring her on this occasion. As I look back now, I see God's hand was already drawing us together.

Through the years, I discovered the friend of my heart. She brought me chicken soup when I was ill, shared books she knew would challenge me, and has spent a small fortune sending cards and notes to delight me. We connected in a way that can best be described as "once in a lifetime."

There is a delicate balance maintained in our relationship, a combination of our strengths and weaknesses, our give and take. It is exciting to toss ideas and plans back and forth and see where we end up. We energize each other.

The differences between us are evident. Cathee wears jewelry like a pro; I forget my clip-on earrings. She forgets things or leaves articles behind, which drives me up a wall, and yet I am not as serious and focused as she would like for me to be. These are big and small irritants that weasel their way into our relationship, but our common goal remains. Working through the distractions and disruptions is the price we pay for our friendship.

I love that Cathee enjoys many of the same things that I do: books, shopping, cards, flowers, travel and dinner parties. It is like having an extension of myself. Even though we live far from each other, she is always close at heart. When the green shades of spring emerge and the flowering crab trees bloom, I want her to see them with me. She loves the fall leaves and crisp air, and I want to share the honking geese with her. I'd love to drag her into the card shop and giggle together over the cards or taste the new recipe I've discovered. Because we are both book junkies, I never finish a good book that I don't want to send it off to her.

Our relationship evolved out of our mutual love for the Lord, our devotion to our husbands and families and friends, respect for one another and our undeniable quest for adventure. Who better to share it with than my pal, Cathee.

The Gift

The table is spread with a colorful French country cloth as three friends and I gather to share a meal and the pure bliss of an afternoon in each other's company. Four gals so diverse, it seems as if we've been caught up together from different parts of the universe. With our eyes sparkling in girlish anticipation, it's as though we've been handed an exquisitely wrapped gift. Yet each of us knows we can't open the package until after our lunch.

We gaze at each other and comment on a stylish haircut, outrageous earrings or a stunning new lip color. Then we laugh and join our hands around the table to give thanks for our friendship. An hour passes in happy occupation as we relish a mouth-watering meal and continue to cast sidelong glances at the imaginary gift before us. We admire the luxurious bow and shiny paper. As coffee is served, we take a closer look at each other—past the kicky haircut, new lipstick, and earrings. We notice that the smile on one friend's face doesn't quite make it to her eyes. An unspoken sadness seems to emanate, so we begin to tug one end of the ribbon, which pulls the bow out of shape and releases its hold on the package. We ask about each other's lives, if anything is stirring our passion lately. As we do, the ribbon slides to a colorful puddle on the floor and the paper is ripped off in one deft movement.

While the box, symbolic of our mutual friendship, contains all the gladness we've shared, it also holds phone calls and emails, some sent out with a plea for help, an urgency to pray. The box is filled with healing and the growth that's taken place in our relationships. We have weathered a few storms and celebrated some triumphs.

Once the box is opened, the dynamics of our friendship emerge in plain view. We've given each other permission to ask hard questions, to listen more than we try to advise, and to provide a safe haven for our friend, who today wears her pain like a shawl draped about her shoulders. Betrayal has flayed open her heart more than once. As a result, trust and vulnerability are not natural for her. Our friendship has offered her a golden vial of healing and forgiveness, but there remains a hesitation in her spirit. We wait, sensing it is an effort to formulate words. Tears start, but still we do nothing. We've learned how to just *be* with each other, not to rescue or fix. We offer her the only thing we have—the gift of our love.

Friendship—a Doorway to Mature Love

The interaction of one friend with another, or a group of friends, is one way God invites us to walk through the door of mature love. While marriage is one form of committed relationship, we find equal commitment in a mutual circle of girlfriends. Giving and receiving love that's wrapped in integrity, without restraint or defense, allows the necessary freedom for growth.

Like a night-blooming jasmine that releases its sweetest fragrance at night, true friends are there when times are difficult. While the friendships we had in our thirties and forties were fun and even challenging, they are nothing like the sacred sisterhood we enjoy now. To open our lives to this small biblical community is to be willing to see ourselves through their eyes, to drop our offenses and our rocks, and to attempt to practice true love for one another. When we recognize that our closest friends are committed to do whatever it takes to spur us on to Christlikeness—that they desire to be led by the Holy Spirit when they speak to us about change and that they are devoted to being honest—that is the moment we grasp that we've taken the word "friend" to a new level.

Expect the Lord to connect you with others who are in line with your purpose and the new path you have chosen for yourself. But don't have any expectations about who they will be. He likes to surprise us. When you feel drawn to someone, watch from a distance and see if her life characterizes the values you hold dear. Be led by His Spirit and let things progress naturally. It's all part of the great adventure.

CHAPTER 10

DANCING TO THE MUSIC
The Beauty of Celebration, Ceremony,
Ritual, and Play

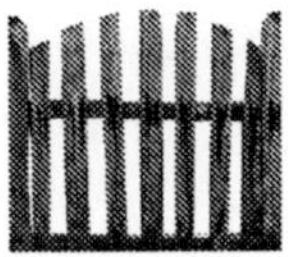

If ever there were people who have cause to celebrate, it is those of us who have shouted yes to God. Entering God's realm of joy, His kingdom, is akin to trading our old clodhoppers for silver dancing shoes. In Romans 14:17, we read these defining words that explain how we'll recognize the true kingdom of God: "For the kingdom of God is...righteousness and peace and joy in the Holy Spirit" (*NKJV*). Who wouldn't want to belong to that realm?

161

We are invited to live our faith in such a way that it becomes a dance instead of a duty. It's a celebration of life that we embrace with our eyes and arms wide open. We must dance to the music the Spirit has deposited in us. And in case you haven't noticed, we don't all hear the same music.

I came across a piece of prose that has circulated around the Internet for a few years. It's called "Dancing with God," and while the author remains anonymous, the message has struck a chord of response and familiarity in almost everyone who reads it.

When I meditated on the word "Guidance," I kept seeing "dance" at the end of the word. I remember reading that doing God's will is a lot like dancing. When two people try to lead, nothing feels right. The movement doesn't flow with the music, and everything is quite uncomfortable and jerky. When one person realizes that, and lets the other lead, both bodies begin to flow with the music. One gives gentle cues, perhaps with a nudge to the back or by pressing lightly in one direction or another. It's as if two become one body, moving beautifully. The dance takes surrender, willingness, and attentiveness from one person, and gentle guidance and skill from the other.

My eyes drew back to the word "Guidance." When I saw "G" I thought of God, followed by "u" and "i." "God," "u" and "i" dance." God, you and I dance.

As I lowered my head, I became willing to trust that I would get guidance about my life. Once again, I became willing to let God lead.

Letting God lead requires our surrender, and until we are willing, He waits out the dance. In His heart, though, is that constant longing to get us on the dance floor. He loves parties, celebrations, weddings, and feasts. Jesus attended them with regularity, and we know He had a good time because of the names people called Him (see Luke 7:34). If we've never learned how to celebrate this life we've been given, it's about time we do.

To what do we surrender when we enter the dance? To God's ways, His Word and His will, of course. That is understood by most. But can we imagine that right before we accept the offer to dance, our Partner asks us a question? How we answer tells Him what He needs to know about the state of our heart. He asks, "Are you willing to be completely at peace with how things are right now in your life? Because in order to dance with Me, to move in sync with My rhythm, you must put aside your discontent, your complaining about how things are, and the anxiety about what's coming. I'm asking for your full trust. These fears direct you to stress and tension. I won't be able to lead you if you are stressed and tense." The surrender He calls for is that we drop all the "what ifs," and respond to His invitation, "Yes, I'd love to dance with You."

Learning How to Dance

Happiness is a choice we make based on our acceptance of how things are in our lives right at this moment. The odd thing is that many of us are not willing to be happy. We fear that if we choose to be happy with our life now—to accept what we can't change—we'll end up stuck or trapped. We are afraid the hand of fate will choose life *for* us if we don't keep striving. As a result we stumble and trip, or else we sit on the sidelines waiting for a better offer, maybe from a different dance partner. We choose not to be happy. A heart afraid of breaking never learns to dance.

Nothing depicts celebration like the dance. We dance at weddings, parties, and reunions. The dance is synonymous with *joie de vivre* and life. So what does it look like when we celebrate the life Jesus has apportioned to us?

I think one of my all-time favorite stories is told by Michael Yaconelli in his book *Dangerous Wonder.* He describes an incident in his childhood when he invited a friend to spend the night. Michael had a stern Italian father who believed that bedtime was for sleeping and nothing else. Nevertheless, the two nine-year-old boys devised a plan to create a "cave" by using blankets to cover the bed so it would be dark as midnight under there. Inside the cave they placed two sleeping bags. They also surrounded the bed with chairs, pillows and lamps and created a secret entrance constructed from coat hangers and towels. This accomplished, they crawled into the sleeping bags where they were to remain trapped in the cave. Being boys with vivid imaginations, however, they weren't content to stay in the cave and soon concocted a plan of escape.

The challenge in this adventure was to keep perfectly quiet so that Dad wouldn't hear them. However, after crawling through the maze and escaping the cave, they decided to start bouncing on the bed. Youth seldom possesses the wisdom to fear consequences. Once into their game, they lost all sense of reason and gave way to what they were—kids playing for all they were worth, oblivious to the thunderous noise they generated. When the door to the bedroom opened suddenly, they gaped in terror as the huge shadow of Dad fell across the room. As Yaconelli relates, "His voice could be heard two houses down: 'GET IN BED *NOW!*'"[38]

Who among us can't remember similar times of wild abandon when we tossed our brains in the air with no thought of consequences? Yet my favorite part of Yaconelli's story is this paragraph:

> I often wonder what would have happened that night if Jesus would have opened the door and caught us jumping on the bed. There is no way to know, of course, but my guess is that Jesus might have looked at us for a moment, laughed, and said, "Move over, guys, I'll show you bouncing!"[39]

Isn't this consistent with Jesus' own words? "I assure you, unless you…become as little children, you will never get into the Kingdom of Heaven" (Matthew 18:3, *NLT*). What if we played as well as prayed people into the kingdom of God?

Simple Play—Deep Play

We live in a culture that thrives on entertainment, but entertainment is not necessarily play. What's the difference? Play is part of every aspect of human life. Courtship includes drama, ritual, and ceremony. Ideas are the result of the mind at play. Language amounts to playing with words. As children, we first begin to test the limits of our environment through play—and who among us didn't test the boundaries as teens? We learn through play. It's also one of the ways we learn to solve problems.

Our God has built play into His universe. Who hasn't watched a litter of kittens tumble and roll with each other, gingerly pawing any object that moves—such as a ball or a butterfly. For us, play is more a refuge from life's monotony, a sanctuary of mind where we are free from the sameness of daily routines.

All play involves risk. In medieval times, games involved ritualized battles between opponents who had spent years developing skill, cunning, and courage. It was a contest to match the abilities of the two contestants. True play involves ritual, action, and unknown outcome. Today, unless we're skydiving, the exposure to hazard is mild. We practice gentler forms of play, but without such play, something within seems to shrivel and die.

This life we are apportioned combines all the elements of true play, deep play. When Jesus bids us enter the narrow gate—in itself a risk because of its constricted space—He is inviting us to take a trip with Him that combines adventure, wonder, ordeal, risk, and fun. Something gnaws within the breast of every human to respond—we are pulled toward the longing for something more than what we have so far experienced. To say yes to following Christ is to respond to the deepest longing in the human heart, the journey of desire, the quest for meaning. It is to enter the romance of life, the dance of the Spirit. Learning to dance to the music, to see beyond the mundane, releases an intense creativity in us.

Simple play can consist in something as effortless as a walk on the beach with a spouse or a friend. At the beach, we may find a unique shell or piece of sea glass that we take home to remind us of salt air and balmy breezes. It sits on our desk, a token that life is beautiful and deserves to be celebrated.

Simple play can also be as elaborate as a dinner party with close friends. Good food, raucous laughter, and perhaps a closing icebreaker at the conclusion of the meal such as, "Describe to us your favorite scene from a movie and tell us why it's your favorite." By the time everyone has shared, we will know more things about each other than we could possibly have drawn out in mere dinner table conversation. Try it sometime.

A Sacred Playground

Play is also able to take us to a place of transcendent awareness, but the requirement is intense focus and awareness. A few years ago, one of my pastors recommended a book that I will cherish the rest of my life. It was a book written by Joseph Jaworski, son of Leon Jaworski, who was the special prosecutor for the Watergate trial. Jaworski's book, *Synchronicity*, was Joe's story, the journey of how his life became a vehicle of learning about true leadership.

In the chapter of his book titled "Oneness," Jaworski touches on the subject of how we learn from animals at play. He describes something that took place on a backpacking trip he made into the Grand Tetons. It was a bright, clear fall day in October, and he rose early that morning to fish a nearby stream close to camp. On his way to the stream, a beautiful ermine appeared in the deep snow. Jaworski describes the scene:

She couldn't have been more than ten feet from me. All at once she appeared with her almost black eyes looking directly into mine. I stopped in my tracks. She sat there staring straight at me, moving not a whisker or a muscle. It seems as if we looked into one another's eyes for several minutes, but perhaps it was less than one. She turned to go but stopped, turned around again, and took another long look at me. Then she began. She jumped up into the air and did a huge flip, and then looked into my eyes again, as if to say, "What did you think about that?" She did this same trick for me three of four times, each time cocking her head to the side and looking at me as it to ask for my approval. I stood there, held transfixed. Then I began smiling and cocking my head in the same direction as hers. This went on for the longest time. There together, I felt at one with that ermine. Finally, when she had finished, she turned around once more and looked at me, then went down into the snow again and was gone.[40]

Jaworski goes on to describe the profoundness of the moment and states that what he experienced was a kind of transcendence of time and space. He understood our oneness with all of God's creation, with all the universe. This is deep play. It comes to us when we are paying attention, listening, and practicing solitude. Almost always, it comes outside our normal routines.

Seeking times of simple play with others or being tuned in enough to capture moments of deep play are choices we are free to make or not make. Our life will go on without such moments, but it becomes shriveled and a poor example of what this life of simple abundance is all about. With nudges from the Holy Spirit, who draws us into the deep game of life, we choose to experience the magnificence of life's special gifts. Annie Dillard put it this way: "The world is fairly studded and strewn with unwrapped gifts and free surprises...cast broadside from a generous hand." Are you unwrapping the gifts He's given you?

Ceremony, Symbol, and Ritual

During the Age of Reason, it appears that evangelicals came to mistrust religious symbolism in the practice of faith. While it seemed appropriate to hold on to the symbol of the cross, all others were suspect. What an enormous loss to our expression of faith.

In its basic sense, a symbol represents a concept or idea. Jesus was a master at the use of metaphor, allegory, and symbol. He called Himself a gate, a door, the bread of heaven, the shepherd, the light of the world. He used reapers to represent angels, seed to portray the Word of God, and types of ground to illustrate the condition of our hearts.

Fran and I have been exploring ways to use symbols in our conference ministry. We have discovered, for instance, the Caim Prayer used by Celtic people of old (see Bro. Tadhg's blog at http://archive.typepad.com/brothertadhg/celtic_stuff/index.html). In this form of prayer, a circle is made with white stones, and the person for whom the prayer is being said stands in the center of the circle (the circle represents the encircling love of God). A group might link arms and stand outside the white stones and pray this prayer over a friend who is troubled:

> Circle ________, Lord
> Keep comfort near and discouragement afar.
> Keep peace within and turmoil out.
> Keep protection near and danger afar.
> Circle ________, Lord
> Keep hope within and despair without.
> Circle ________, Lord
> Keep peace within and anxiety without
> Circle ________, Lord
> Keep light near and darkness afar.
> May the peace of all peace be Yours tonight,
> To shield you, ________, on every side.
> In the name of the eternal Father, Son, and Holy Spirit.
> Amen.

The beauty of this ceremony often causes us, as well as the person in the circle, to weep. We have touched heaven for a moment. We've experienced a symbolic way of picturing the surrounding love and grace of the Lord. At the conclusion of the ceremony, we often give the person for whom we prayed a white stone as a remembrance of God's faithfulness and protection and as a way for her to recall the prayer of those who interceded on her behalf. We do this based on Jesus' words in Revelation 2:17: "And I will give him a white stone, and on the stone a new name written which no one knows except him who receives it" (*NKJV*).

Another beautiful ritual that can be used in small groups, retreats, or any type of gathering is to fill a large shallow stone, copper, or wooden bowl filled with water and place it on a pedestal or small table. Give each participant a stone (you can use the small stones that are sold in craft stores to anchor candles in large glass hurricanes). At the conclusion of a short teaching on letting go, each person brings her stone as a symbol of something she wishes to release to God. She simply places it in the water and walks back to her seat.

It seems we fear the words "ritual," "ceremony," and "symbol," because in ages past the Church practiced many forms of tradition that amounted to form without substance. The question is whether we can't have form *with* substance. Postmodernism is upon us, and we have left the Age of Reason. Today's followers of Christ are hungry and thirsty for authentic ways to experience His teachings and their faith. The days of ordered rows of people listening to lecture-type sermons are virtually over. Writing our prayer requests on Post-It Notes and sticking them to a wooden cross are more meaningful to us today than calling the church office and having our request placed on the prayer list. This is especially true when, at the end of the gathering, someone goes to the cross and takes our prayer home with them to pray for us during the week. This is biblical community.

There are moments when I practice something I call "stopping." It's my own ritual for paying attention to my life and to what's going on inside and around me. Many times, I simply stop what I'm doing, slip out to the back porch, and curl up in a deck chair to observe what's out there in that moment. Maybe it's a bright red cardinal at the feeder that is quickly challenged by a shiny black crow, and I notice the striking contrast of their colors. Or maybe the lonchocarpus trees are sporting their purple spikes, releasing a fragrance similar to lilacs, and the breeze passes over as though an imaginary hand strokes them. Or perhaps butterflies—yellow, black and orange, or even pure white—hover around the blooms. It's quiet except for a lawn mover off in the distance. I realize in that moment that I'm happy and life is good.

We can use any routine we carry out mindlessly as an opportunity to express our connection with God. Standing at the microwave warming coffee can be a 30-second ritual of thanking God for the morning's work and offering it as a sacrifice to Him. Preparing a pot of tea takes a bit longer, but provides opportunity to bless the earth and its produce—the tea, in this case. As the boiling water on the tea leaves releases an aroma, we are reminded that our prayers rise to God as incense, or that our lives are a "sweet smelling savor" to Him.

Anniversaries of the Heart

Henry Wadsworth Longfellow wrote, "The holiest of all holidays are those kept by ourselves in silence and apart, the secret anniversaries of the heart." Do not fear the repetition of ritual. In our over-analytical society, there is a comfort in repeating things we learn by heart: the Lord's Prayer, the Twenty-Third Psalm, the Apostles' Creed. What are hymns and praise songs if they are not the repetition of our beliefs set to music?

The practice of ceremony and ritual enables us to enter a holy arena. Without it, we find life too complicated and too exhausting to live. Ceremony refreshes and centers us. As the Shabbat candles are lit each Friday at twilight, the peace of familiar ritual still quiets the hearts of Jewish families today. The work week is over, and it's time to remember the source of all health, provision, peace, and love.

Halloween is a living reminder that some ceremonies continue long after the reason for them no longer exists. Originally, this event signaled the end of the harvest, the last slaughter of animals to store up for meat during the long difficult winters. Piles of apples, pumpkins and winter squash, wheat and barley grains all stored neatly in granaries, root cellars and barns. There was also blood, however, and bones to burn. Somehow, in pre-Christian Ireland, where Halloween is said to have started, Druids turned the gore into superstition. Even after the gospel came to the Emerald Isles, the inhabitants held on to the folklore.

How beautiful today to see the true meaning restored—the Harvest Festivals at churches, homes decorated with pumpkins and scarecrows, fall wreaths on the doors. Even in Florida, where there is virtually little change of season, the expressions of God's bounty are demonstrated.

What couple doesn't know, even if they fail to participate, that the ritual of a weekly date helps to keep the passion alive? There's a joy in getting all dolled up for a date, planning what to wear, selecting the restaurant, and preparing how the rest of the evening will unfold.

How many of us have welcomed the New Year at a watch-night service where we gather around 10 P.M. for a late supper, play games, and celebrate a brand-new opportunity to start over again? At 11:30, a quieter mood settles over the group. As the children drift off to sleep on the floor, we gather to sing praises to God for His goodness during the past 12 months. Toward midnight, we begin to pray out the old year and pray in the new.

Perhaps your creativity will blossom this year and you'll gather with friends around a fire. On a scrap of paper, those in the group will write out their hopes for the coming year. After a time of silent prayer, one by one they'll drop the papers into the red hot flames and watch them turn to ash as little sparks of light dance off into the black sky and carry hopes and dreams for better things straight up to the heavens.

The first New Year's Eve that Fran and I spent together was at my house in Lake Placid, Florida. We enjoyed a relaxed morning on the deck, sipping fresh-ground coffee with Bob and Bill, surrounded by live oaks that dripped grey-green Spanish moss like old ladies with silver hair. Lake Clay spread out before us as we watched a great blue heron stalk his prey from the edge of the aquatic lily patch, while a little egret landed on the dock. We even watched in wonder as a 6-foot alligator cruised down the center of the lake.

In the evening, we prepared a sumptuous supper that the four of us shared in glowing candlelight as we talked about the events of that year. Close to midnight, we prepared elements for communion and prayed—thanking God for all we'd come through and speaking our deepest heart desires for what was to come. Then, in reverent ceremony, we observed the Lord's Supper together.

We have celebrated Communion—the most sacred of all rituals of the church—in homes, at the beach, and once even on a boat with a group of women who spent the weekend at an island cottage to plan an upcoming retreat.

Common Rituals

We celebrate and commemorate the moments of our lives in rituals. Whether a birth, death, marriage, or graduation, our way of marking the moment is through ceremony. How else can we explain a bride wearing white or the wedding ring worn on the third finger of the left hand or the graduate wearing a cap and gown? We celebrate the arrival of a new life by showering the mother-to-be with gifts and necessities to aid her in caring for the baby. Fraternities and sororities practice rituals of acceptance or tests of devotion. Baptism is a sacred observance that the person is being identified with Christ and the company of the redeemed.

We need ceremony because it gives value and meaning to our rites of passage, our losses and gains, and the otherwise ordinariness of our lives. Ritual raises these events to levels of importance or sacredness. They help restore our souls and bring order when difficulties come and when we feel things are spinning into the universe of bewilderment. They allow us to feel less helpless.

I recall one such moment when we lived in Key West and a close friend of ours named Ben lost his job. It came unexpected and jarred him, his family, and us—his circle of friends. After talking among ourselves, we called and invited him and his wife out to dinner at one of our favorite restaurants. Before the customary blessing over the food, my husband stood at the head of the table and with a broad grin said, "Ben, we have gathered today to celebrate your new promotion." We all laughed and applauded. Then we prayed for Ben and his family and celebrated the new course the Lord set him on.

Oh, how much we have to celebrate. How many lovely things there are in life to mark.

CHAPTER 11

FINDING THE KEY
TO THE GARDEN
Where Mysteries Come into View

Mary looked at it, not really knowing why the hole was there, and as she looked she saw something almost buried in the newly-turned soil. It was something like a ring of rusty iron or brass and…she put out her hand and picked the ring up. It was more than a ring, however; it was an old key which looked as if it had been buried a long time…. "Perhaps it has been buried for ten years," she said in a whisper. "Perhaps it is the key to the garden."[41]
—Frances Hodgson Burnett, *The Secret Garden*

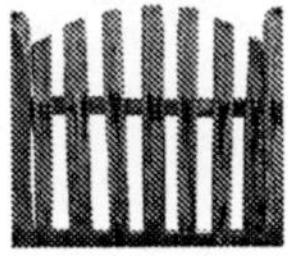

And the LORD *God planted a garden eastward in Eden; and there he put the man whom he had formed.*
—Genesis 2:8, *KJV*

A garden enclosed is my sister, my spouse; a spring shut up, a fountain sealed.
—Song of Solomon 4:12, *KJV*

And he showed me a pure river of water of life, clear as crystal, proceeding from the throne of God and of the Lamb. In the middle of its street, and on either side of the river, was the tree of life, which bore twelve fruits, each tree yielding its fruit every month.
—Revelation 22:1-2, *NKJV*

The story of mankind begins in a garden and ends in a garden. It begins with a man, a woman, and a wedding and ends with the same. (God is, after all, a hopeless romantic.) For those who call themselves Christ-followers, the garden is a picture of home.

The word "home" creates a mental image that speaks to the heart. While a picture is worth a thousand words, it is not merely the visual picture that speaks. Visual images are used to trigger mental images. It's the mental image we're after. It's the same goal of fiction writers, authors of movie scripts, artists, musicians, and architects. The goal is always to trigger the mental image.

In His writing, God uses mental images to convey powerful thoughts that cause us to see into another realm. The scriptures quoted above link two ideas: *garden* and *home.* These words conjure up all sorts of mental images. A garden speaks of a private, lush, secret place—or at least it does if we search out its origins in the original Hebrew. It is where we began life, but also where we lost what had been bequeathed to us. The entire Bible is the story of that loss and the mission of Jesus to redeem what was stolen, to bring us back to the place where everything is restored. We are on our way home.

It is virtually impossible to translate the English word "home" into other tongues. The mixture of memory and longing, security, inclusiveness, and love defy translation into a single word. It is not at all the same, for instance, as the word "house."

Roy Williams, who writes a weekly blog called "The Monday Morning Memo," says this about home:

Home is a concept, not a place; it's a state of mind where self-definition starts. It is origins, a mix of time and place and smell and weather wherein one first realizes one is an original…. Home is where one first learned to be separate, and it remains in the mind as the place where reunion, if it were ever to occur, would happen. All literary romance, all romance epic, derives from the Odyssey and it is about going home.

Home is where we started and home is where we'll end up. For us, home is a garden.

Our personal narrative emerges as part of a glorious drama consisting of two congruent stories: the story of a God who is seeking a resting place, a home; and the story of God as an ageless romantic consumed with the pursuit of a bride. These truths were shrouded in mystery until now, but we have been chosen to give visible expression to the fact that another realm has invaded this planet to bring a message of love and hope. God is crazy, head over heels in love with us, and everything that was lost in the first three chapters of Genesis will be restored in the last three chapters of Revelation. Can it get any better than that?

The Love of God's Life

Song of Solomon has long baffled students, teachers, and masters of Bible study. It is far too sensual for most people to relate it to God. It has the audacity to claim in the opening paragraph to be the song above all songs—the greatest love song ever written or sung, and it is written about two lovers. Because the theme of God pursuing a bride for His Son weaves itself throughout the pages of Scripture, we don't have to stretch too far to conclude that this book of the Bible is about Jesus' great love, the Church.

But what *is* the Church? Better yet, *who* is the Church? Ephesians 5 speaks to us of another mysterious union, one that takes place between a man and his wife and is a picture of Christ and His church (see v. 32).

It's another mental image with astounding implications. The Church that is spoken of in that passage is not a building.

It was Augustine who said that if God is love, there must be within Him a lover, a beloved. The mystery kept secret through the ages is that just as God opened Adam's side and took out a part from which He fashioned Adam's counterpart—a woman—so God opened His Son Jesus' side and from it has fashioned another bride—the Body of Christ, the Church. The Church is comprised of people known as the Bride of Christ because, just like Eve, they come from His side, are a new creation and love Him passionately because their love comes from Him. This is the mystery revealed.

You, dear one, are the Bride of Christ. You are part of a company— men and women, boys and girls—who have responded to the love of the Bridegroom. When we give our hearts to Him and surrender to His passionate love, we become His Bride.

What a mystery story! Who could ever have guessed that all the points of Adam and Eve's story would find their counterpoint in the story of Christ and His Bride. As Adam named all the animals and saw that they each had an "other"—like them but different—he must have wondered where his own counterpart was. He felt great passion in his heart and had nowhere to express it until God gave him a bride.

The woman (she wasn't called "Eve" until after the Fall) wasn't a part of the seven days of creation. She was hidden in Adam until the eighth day—the day of new beginnings. She was part of the new creation. She is Adam, but in another form. She was shaped out of Adam's substance and was his glory, for as Paul tells us in 1 Corinthians 11:7, "The woman is the glory of the man."

Could there ever be a more dramatic love story that this? Can you see how all things are unfolding toward this great completion of what began in the first garden and will consummate in the last garden? The Bride is destined to become the Wife—the love of God's life.

Portals to the Unseen

Portals move us between the *this* and the *that*—from old opinions to new ones, from the unknown to the known, from darkness to light. The greatest portal, the one between life and death, earth and heaven, was the portal Jesus opened from here to eternity. When He flung open that door the first Easter, He made it possible for us to leave our self-centered natures and become part of His new creation.

We see evidence of portals in music, literature, and architecture, and we have looked at a variety of these portals throughout the chapters of this book. Both books and movies transport us to realms of understanding that surpass conversation. In the movie, *The Matrix*, for instance, Neo's red pill has the power to unveil the truth. He is told, "You take the red pill, you stay in Wonderland, and I show you how deep the rabbit-hole goes." The red pill is a portal, and Morpheus's words are a reference to yet another portal in literature—the rabbit hole in *Alice in Wonderland*. In *The Lion the Witch and the Wardrobe*, Lucy enters the wardrobe portal and ends up in Narnia. In *The Wizard of Oz*, Dorothy is whisked away in a tornado portal and finds herself in Oz. The question we must ask ourselves is, "Am I ready for Narnia? Will I swallow the red pill?"

We can choose to view these as silly fantasy stories and fairy tales, or we can see them as deeper explanations of the meaning of life. Myths, fairy tales, and fantasies help us understand concepts that are not easily understood in the natural. The truth is, things are not always as they seem. We are invited by God to see into His realm. In fact, He tells us to focus on that realm. He explains that there are other ways to experience life than just the five senses; there is truly a sixth sense. Viewing life through the portals of music, story, shapes (such as windows, gates, doors and paths), colors, symbols, and rituals encourages us to enter the mysteries of God. "So we fix our eyes not on what is seen, but on what is unseen. For what is seen is temporary, but what is unseen is eternal" (2 Corinthians 4:18, *NIV*).

When Mary Lennox found the long-lost, rusty key to the secret garden and placed it in the lock, she entered a portal that had been shut for 10 years. If you've ever read the children's book, *The Secret Garden*, you'll remember that a fall happened there, and because of it the garden was sealed. It's reminiscent of another fall in a garden where we read, "He threw them out of the garden and stationed angel-cherubim and a revolving sword of fire east of it, guarding the path to the Tree-of-Life" (Genesis 3:24, *THE MESSAGE*).

God removed Adam and Eve from the Garden of Eden not out of anger but because of love. They ate the fruit of the Tree of the Knowledge of Good and Evil, but they had not yet tasted the fruit from the Tree of Life. If they had, they would have been eternally separated from God in their fallen state. So He drove them out and sealed up the garden. However, when we read Revelation 22:2, the Tree of Life reappears. The mental image snaps quickly into place: we are going back to that garden; we will reenter that portal from which we have been barred all these centuries.

Pilgrims of the Heart

Our lives, with all their joys, battles, sorrows, and victories, are one long pilgrimage. We are pilgrims of the heart, living with the sweet ache for something beyond what we've experienced so far. If we reflect with any honesty at all, we must admit that periodically, at the strangest moments, we have heard the haunting call of a voice that beckons us to follow—to step outside our tidy, circumscribed box and fall into His adventure.

Fran and I know you have heard the call, too, and that you've also considered casting aside your rational fears to see where the road may lead. You would never have made it to this chapter otherwise. It is to you who have ears to hear that the mysterious summons has been issued. You are not a wanderer but a wayfarer, a pilgrim. Wanderers don't know where they're going. Pilgrims do.

Be encouraged that God is *for* you and not *against* you. In fact, He promises to honor your quest: "Blessed are those whose strength is in you, who have set their hearts on pilgrimage" (Psalm 84:5, *NIV*). He even says He will "shower blessings on the pilgrims who come here, and give supper to those who arrive hungry" (Psalm 132:15, *NIV*). When the hunger inside of us cries out, "There's more!" He is ready to feed us with spiritual food the world cannot offer.

One of God's deepest desires is to reveal Himself to you in a personal way and to awaken you to the core of who you are. The thresholds and passages along which you've journeyed have enabled you to choose to live without resignation and to come to a place of deep acceptance. These thresholds and passages have shown you the path to serenity, the futility of living a frenzied life that precludes reflection and holy leisure. You've seen the importance of letting go, not just of all the things you cannot change of your past and its failures, but also of all the lies that say you aren't God's beloved. You are letting go and letting come—taking hold of today, NOW, the precious present.

Learning to embrace your false self has enabled you to let Jesus restore the broken parts of your soul that seemed crushed and scattered to the winds. When He did that for you, your true self was able to emerge, joyful and free. Your pilgrimage has led you to uncover a bouquet of ways to nurture the freedom you've won—healthy, fun friendships, the practice of solitude, the importance of play, celebration and ritual traditions of the heart. You have ventured into a land of dangerous wonder, attempting to begin an awkward dance that will turn into a graceful ballet.

Living an Outrageous Life

I remember the fall of 1952. I grew up in the city of Miami, Florida, close to what is now called "Little Havana." But in those days, Fidel Castro was nowhere in sight and our neighborhood primarily consisted of American kids who longed for the woods, a place to be wild and free. At the end of SW 6th Street, where I lived, if you made a sharp left turn at 30th Avenue, you came to the only spot we could call our own. It was a circle that provided a hub for 4th, 5th, and 6th Streets. Around the perimeter of this circle, which I imagine was about 100 feet wide, were Florida native mahogany trees. We climbed those trees so often that I'm surprised there were any limbs left. We'd pass each other in the hall of Auburndale Elementary School and whisper, "Meet you at the circle after school."

That particular fall, the tree trimmers came to trim all the mahogany trees in the circle. To our utter delight, they left the cut branches in two huge piles on either side of the circumference. The lines were drawn. The trucks were barely out sight before we were in the middle, choosing sides. We built elaborate forts with tunnels in which we stored the only ammunition we could find during that season—pinecones.

With recklessness, we conducted pinecone fights every day until dusk fell and we heard our mothers' voices summoning us to the dinner table. We were so completely obsessed with this war that it's amazing any of us passed to the sixth grade. All day long we daydreamed of new strategies and wistfully gazed out the classroom window, counting the minutes until the final bell. The battles lasted into December, when to our horror we arrived one afternoon to find the circle neatly cleared of all the limbs.

That was my first experience with passionate, reckless living. It would be more than 40 years before I came back to that place and understood for the first time that Jesus didn't instruct me to play it safe. He didn't say, "Follow my rules." He said, "Follow Me." He loves us with a passion of wild, dangerous intensity. We are His magnificent obsession. He risked everything not to teach us to live right but to make it possible for us to live fully.

The kind of life we're called to presses us to invest all our possessions, not to bury them in the ground and play it safe. That guy that Jesus mentioned in one of His parables, the one who buried his talent, was the only one of three who drew scorn from God. God smiles on risk takers. We've spent so many of our years buried under the theology and apologetics of Christianity that we've missed the whole intent of God's heart—to live vibrant, enthusiastic lives of passion and carelessness. Yes, carelessness! He said, "Be careful for nothing," didn't He?

What is the Key to the Garden?

"A garden enclosed is my sister, my spouse; a spring shut up, a fountain sealed" (Song of Solomon 4:12, *KJV*). This is the secret place where my lover waits. The lover of my soul. The one who knows everything about me because He created me. I am not a happenstance, an accident, or a product of fate. I am the Beloved.

The key that unlocks the door into the secret garden, the enclosed meeting place of lovers, can only be love. Love is the key. We love Him because He first loved us. That's how we got the key in the first place. This speaks of a personal, intimate relationship. The Bible never gives us a nebulous message that we are to be one with the universe. No, we are one—just as a man and woman come together in holy union—with Jesus Christ who was, and is, and ever will be. Our union with Him transcends the physical and makes us one: body, soul, and spirit.

Jesus is a real person, not the religious figment of someone's imagination. He loves us madly, passionately, intimately, and even obsessively. How can you say otherwise when you read these words: "You've captured my heart…you looked at me, and I fell in love. One look my way and I was hopelessly in love!" (Song of Solomon 4:9, *THE MESSAGE*).

The Life We Were Meant to Live

You are on a journey that will eventually take you home. C.S. Lewis put it this way:

At present we are on the outside of the world, the wrong side of the door. We discern the freshness and purity of morning, but they do not make us fresh and pure. We cannot mingle with the splendours we see. But all the leaves of the New Testament are rustling with the rumour that it will not always be so. Some day, God willing, we shall get *in*.[42]

In the meantime, we have a life to live here and now. Although we are slightly uncomfortable because this isn't home, we still know this part of the journey is not meant to be a middle-of-the-road, play-it-safe, boringly predictable trip. It is meant to be beyond-the-imagination, over-the-top, and explosively joyous. Of all people on earth, we are meant to savor the taste of real life. We catch glimpses into the other realm from time to time, and these give us hope to continue on toward the end. In her allegory about our journey toward home, *Hind's Feet on High Places,* Hannah Hurnard shows us an inward glance to the truth:

When you continue your journey there may be much mist and cloud. Perhaps it may even seem as though everything you have seen here of the high places was just a dream, or the work of your own imagination.... But you have seen *reality*, and the mist which seems to swallow it up is the illusion. Believe steadfastly in what you have seen. Even if the way up to the high places appears to be obscured and you are led to doubt whether you are following the right path, remember the promise, "Thine ears shall hear a word behind thee, saying, This is the way, walk ye in it, when ye turn to the right hand and when ye turn to the left." Always go forward along the path of obedience as far as you know it until I intervene, even if it seems to be leading you where you fear I could never mean you to go.

Real life, of course, includes pain, sorrow, disappointment, failure, and loss. The twists and turns, however, are put in the road to teach us to trust the one we follow, to rely on His strength and not our own, to believe in His declared love to the point that we rest in the assurance of it. Real life is only attained by authentic and vulnerable people who have decided that following Jesus is worth the risk. Have you decided to be one of those people?

Our paradigm shifts once we see that we are not citizens of this world trying to make our way to heaven but are citizens of heaven trying to make our way through this world. Our lives are not about earning God's love and favor. We already have that because we are His Beloved. No, we are called to live as children of a kingdom that will change everything, heirs to an inheritance we can already taste, and a company of redeemed living the life we were meant to live.

It's as though Jesus speaks the words of this poem as His invitation for us to live with a sense of awe in the beauty of our days and to anticipate the glory of what is yet to come. You are once again at a crossroads. If you turn back now, there is only what might have been.

THE EXPLORER

Meet me where the shadows end
Where reason melts and time can bend
Where thrills explode and magic runs
And hope shines brighter in the sun
It's a place where eyes can barely see
But a heart can fathom perfectly
It's where ideas soar and fly
With silver wings up in the sky
Where nothing's scripted, all is new
And mysteries come into view
Meet me outside logic's door,
Come with me, we will explore
Meet me in the golden sea
Where dreams begin
It's where I'll be[43]

ENDNOTES

Chapter 1

1. Ken Gire, *Windows of the Soul: Experiencing God in New Ways* (Grand Rapids, MI: Zondervan Publishing House, 1996), p. 23.

2. Tom Schulman, *Dead Poet's Society*, Directed by Peter Weir, (Touchstone Pictures, 1989).

3. Roy H. Williams, "Monday Morning Memo," mondaymorningmemo.com.

4. Sue Monk Kidd, *The Mermaid Chair* (New York: Penguin Group, 2005), p. 1.

5. Michael Yaconelli, *Dangerous Wonder* (Colorado Springs, CO: Navpress, 1998, 2003).

Chapter 2

6. Dan Allender, *The Cry of the Soul* (Colorado Springs, CO: Navpress, 1994), pp. 37-38.

7. Jodi Picoult, *Vanishing Acts* (New York: Washington Square Press, 2005).

8. Ken Gire, *Windows of the Soul: Experiencing God in New Ways* (Grand Rapids, MI: Zondervan Publishing House, 1996), p. 72.

9. Brennan Manning, *Ruthless Trust* (New York: Nan A. Talese, 1995).

Chapter 3

10. Anne Morrow Lindbergh, *Gift from the Sea* (New York: Pantheon Books, 1991).

Chapter 4

11. Brent Curtis and John Eldredge, *The Sacred Romance: Drawing Closer to the Heart of God* (Nashville, TN: Thomas Nelson, 1997).

12. Ranier Maria Rilke, *Letters to a Young Poet* (Novato, CA: New World Library, 2000), p. 35.

13. C.S. Lewis, *The Letters of C.S. Lewis,* 21 December 1941, para. 3, p. 197.

14. Ken Gire, *Windows of the Soul: Experiencing God in New Ways* (Grand Rapids: Zondervan Publishing House, 1996), p. 72.

Chapter 5

15. Foster, *Celebration of Discipline* (New York: HarperCollins, 1978), p. 27.

16. Dan Allender, *The Cry of the Soul* (Colorado Springs, CO: Navpress, 1994).

17. Larry Crabb, *Shattered Dreams: God's Unexpected Pathway to Joy* (Colorado Springs, CO: WaterBrook Press, 2002).

18. Ibid.

Chapter 6

19. Brent Curtis and John Eldredge, *The Sacred Romance: Drawing Closer to the Heart of God* (Nashville, TN: Thomas Nelson, 1997), p. 149.
20. Sue Monk Kidd, *When the Heart Waits: Spiritual Direction for Life's Sacred Questions* (San Francisco: HarperCollins, 1990), p. 101.
21. Frederick Buechner, *The Eyes of the Heart* (San Francisco: HarperSanFrancisco, 1999), pp. 93-94.
22. Lucy M. Montgomery, *Anne of Green Gables* (New York: L.C. Page & Co., 1908).
23. Ken Gire, *Windows of the Soul: Experiencing God in New Ways* (Grand Rapids, MI: Zondervan, 1996), p. 81.

Chapter 7

24. Ken Gire, *Windows of the Soul: Experiencing God in New Ways* (Grand Rapids, MI: Zondervan, 1996), p. 22.
25. John Eldredge and Brent Curtis, *The Sacred Romance* (Nashville, TN: Thomas Nelson, 1997).
26. Sue Monk Kidd, *When the Heart Waits: Spiritual Direction for Life's Sacred Questions* (San Francisco: HarperCollins, 1990).
27. Oriah Mountain Dreamer, *The Dance: Moving to the Rhythms of Your True Self* (New York: HarperCollins, 2001), p. xii.

Chapter 8

28. Ken Gire, *The Reflective Life* (Colorado Springs, CO: Chariot Victor Publishing, 1998), p. 97.
29. Sue Monk Kidd, *When the Heart Waits* (San Francisco: HarperCollins 1992), p. 126.
30. Frederick Buechner, *Sacred Journey* (New York: HarperCollins, 1982), p. 77.

31. Christina Baldwin, *Life's Companion: Journal Writing as a Spiritual Quest* (New York: Bantam Books, 1991), p. 18.

32. Janice Elsheimer, *The Creative Call: An Artist's Response to the Way of the Spirit* (Colorado Springs, CO: WaterBrook Press, 2001).

33. Adapted from www.writingthejourney.com.

Chapter 9

34. Ibid.

35. Lucy M. Montgomery, *Anne of Green Gables* (New York: L.C. Page & Co., 1908), p. 56.

36. Laurie Beth Jones, *Jesus CEO* (New York: Hyperion, 1995), p. 221.

37. Sue Monk Kidd, *The Mermaid Chair* (New York: Penguin Group, 2005).

Chapter 10

38. Sue Monk Kidd, *When the Heart Waits* (San Francisco: HarperCollins 1992).

39. Ibid.

40. Ibid., p. 73.

41. Joseph Jaworski, *Synchronicity: The Inner Path of Leadership* (San Francisco: Berett-Koehler Publishers), p. 52.

Chapter 11

42. Frances Hodgson Burnett, *The Secret Garden* (New York: J. B. Lippincott, 1911) p. 65.

43. C.S. Lewis, *The Weight of Glory* (San Francisco: HarperSanFrancisco, 2001).

44. Hannah Hurnard, *Hinds' Feet on High Places* (Carol Stream, IL: Tyndale House, 1975), p. 189.

45. Kim N. Poulsen, "The Explorer," 2001.

To order additional copies of this title call:
1-877-421-READ (7323)
or please visit our Web site at
www.pleasantwordbooks.com

If you enjoyed this quality custom-published book,

drop by our Web site for more books and information.

www.winepressgroup.com

"Your partner in custom publishing."

To contact the authors or book a conference visit:
www.thresholdsandpassages.com
www.thresholdsandpassages.blogspot.com
franlankford@thresholdsandpassages.com
catheepoulsen@thresholdsandpassages.com

Printed in the United States
200785BV00010B/77/A